Global Networks and Innovation in China

T0299744

After almost twenty years of internationalization, Chinese firms have shown their growing innovation capability through benefiting from global networks and domestic efforts. However, how Chinese firm innovation is facilitated at the international and domestic levels remains to be understood.

This book investigates innovation in China from three aspects. First, starting at the international level, the effects of Chinese–foreign linkages in innovation are examined from the relationship view and the foreign ownership perspective. Second, before moving to the domestic level, the moderating role of global networks (e.g., global supply chain collaboration) is examined to understand the relationship between competition of unregistered firms and innovation of registered firms. Third, at the domestic level, innovation is studied from both upstream and downstream of the value chain: consumers' decision-making in innovative products and strategic choices, and environment constraints for product innovation.

Collectively, this book actively investigates innovation in China at international and domestic levels. It investigates how the global networks contribute to innovation in China and how domestic Chinese firms strengthen their innovation capability. The volume, thus, makes an important attempt to extend existing knowledge on this subject and provides new insights to scholars and practitioners.

The chapters in this book were originally published as a special issue of *International Studies of Management & Organization*.

Tian Wei is Professor in School of Management, Fudan University. Her research interests cover cross-border acquisitions and corporate social entrepreneurship. She has published in leading management journals, including *Journal of Management Studies* and *British Journal of Management*. She has served as an editor for *Management and Organization Review*, and *Asian Case Research Journal*.

Maoliang Bu is Associate Professor at Nanjing University. He has published in leading academic journals including *Journal of International Business Studies* (*JIBS*) and *Strategic Management Journal* (*SMJ*). He has served as an editor for *Journal of Business Ethics*, *Asia Pacific Journal of Management*, and *Journal of International Management*.

Global Networks and Innovation in China

International Linkages and Indigenous Efforts

Edited by
Tian Wei and Maoliang Bu

LONDON AND NEW YORK

First published 2022
by Routledge
2 Park Square, Milton Park, Abingdon, Oxon OX14 4RN

and by Routledge
605 Third Avenue, New York, NY 10158

Routledge is an imprint of the Taylor & Francis Group, an informa business

© 2022 Taylor & Francis

British Library Cataloguing in Publication Data
A catalogue record for this book is available from the British Library

ISBN: 978-0-367-77139-3 (hbk)
ISBN: 978-0-367-77140-9 (pbk)
ISBN: 978-1-003-16995-6 (ebk)

Typeset in Times New Roman
by Newgen Publishing UK

Publisher's Note
The publisher accepts responsibility for any inconsistencies that may have arisen during the conversion of this book from journal articles to book chapters, namely the inclusion of journal terminology.

Disclaimer
Every effort has been made to contact copyright holders for their permission to reprint material in this book. The publishers would be grateful to hear from any copyright holder who is not here acknowledged and will undertake to rectify any errors or omissions in future editions of this book.

Contents

Citation Information

The chapters in this book were originally published in the *International Studies of Management & Organization*, volume 49, issue 2 (2019). When citing this material, please use the original page numbering for each article, as follows:

Introduction

Global Networks and Innovation in China—International Linkages and Indigenous Efforts
Tian Wei and Maoliang Bu
International Studies of Management & Organization, volume 49, issue 2 (2019) pp. 121–125

Chapter 1

Innovation Through Linkage, Leverage, and Learning: The Case of Monk Fruit Corporation
Joanna Scott-Kennel, Haolin Yin and Michele E. M. Akoorie
International Studies of Management & Organization, volume 49, issue 2 (2019) pp. 126–150

Chapter 2

Foreign Ownership and External Knowledge Acquisition: A Comparison between International Subsidiaries and Local Firms in China
Zhi Yang and Tian Wei
International Studies of Management & Organization, volume 49, issue 2 (2019) pp. 151–172

Chapter 3

How Does Competition By Informal Firms Affect The Innovation In Formal Firms?
Jorge A. Heredia Pérez, Xiaohua Yang, Ou Bai, Alejandro Flores and Walter Heredia Heredia
International Studies of Management & Organization, volume 49, issue 2 (2019) pp. 173–190

Chapter 4

Applying Complexity Theory To Understand Chinese Consumers' Decision-Making In Innovative Products

Zhe Zhang, Yuansi Hou and Yongmin Zhu

International Studies of Management & Organization, volume 49, issue 2 (2019) pp. 191–212

Chapter 5

Success Factors for Product Innovation in China's Manufacturing Sector: Strategic Choice and Environment Constraints

Zhenzhong Ma and Quan Jin

International Studies of Management & Organization, volume 49, issue 2 (2019) pp. 213–231

For any permission-related enquiries please visit:
www.tandfonline.com/page/help/permissions

Notes on Contributors

Michele E. M. Akoorie, ICL Graduate Business School, Auckland, New Zealand.

Ou Bai, School of Tourism and Health Management, Zhejiang A&F University, Hangzhou, P. R. China.

Maoliang Bu, Business School and Hopkins-Nanjing Center, Nanjing University, Nanjing, P. R. China.

Alejandro Flores, Universidad del Pacífico, Lima, Perú.

Walter Heredia Heredia, Universidad del Pacífico, Lima, Perú.

Jorge Heredia Pérez, Universidad del Pacífico, Lima, Perú.

Yuansi Hou, School of Business and Management, Queen Mary University of London, London, UK.

Quan Jin, School of Business, Shanghai University of International Business and Economics, Shanghai, China.

Zhenzhong Ma, Odette School of Business, University of Windsor, Windsor, Ontario, Canada.

Joanna Scott-Kennel, Waikato Management School, University of Waikato, Hamilton, New Zealand.

Tian Wei, Department of Business Administration, School of Management, Fudan University, Shanghai, P. R. China.

Xiaohua Yang, School of Management, University of San Francisco, Moral Culture Research Center Hunan Normal University, San Francisco, CA, USA.

Zhi Yang, Huazhong University of Science and Technology, Wuhan, P. R. China.

Haolin Yin, Waikato Management School, University of Waikato, Hamilton, New Zealand.

Zhe Zhang, School of Management, Fudan University, Shanghai, P. R. China.

Yongmin Zhu, International School of Business & Finance, Sun Yat-sen University, Guangzhou, P. R. China.

Introduction

Global Networks and Innovation in China—International Linkages and Indigenous Efforts

Tian Wei and Maoliang Bu

Abstract: After almost twenty years of internationalization, Chinese firms have demonstrated their ability to benefit from both international linkages and indigenous efforts in product and process innovation. However, how Chinese firm innovation is facilitated at the international and domestic levels remains to be understood. This article provides an overview of our special issue, exploring this important topic of global networks and innovation in China. Through five empirical studies employing a variety of research methods (e.g., case study, secondary data, survey, and fuzzy-set analysis), we present some recent research on balancing and manipulating internal and external networks to enhance Chinese firm innovation. These selected articles contribute to the field of networks and innovation in China. We hope these articles play a role in encouraging further research on this important and interesting field.

As an emerging economy, China has quickly risen up the global rankings in a number of knowledge-intensive sectors. This well-recognized climb up the global rankings has demonstrated the growing innovation capability of Chinese firms. However, recently, there is business news that ZTE Corporation faced paralysis if any American businesses stopped selling their products or services to it. This news makes scholars and practitioners aware that the innovation capability of Chinese firms may not be as strong as perceived. Even though China's innovation capability is under controversy, the Chinese government has shown its ambition to enhance firm innovation. For example, the "Belt and Road" initiative facilitates foreign-invested innovation through extended global networks, and the "popular entrepreneurship and mass innovation" initiative encourages the domestic innovation of each individual.

Internationally, multinational corporations (MNCs) have largely invested their R&D in China, and the R&D centers diffuse knowledge to both local and international markets (Deng

2003; Fan 2006). From ownership advantage theory, MNCs transfer advanced proprietary technology, immobile strategic assets (e.g., brands, local distribution networks), and other capabilities, to their subsidiaries (Li and Zhong 2003; Warner et al. 2004; Zhang 2003). As their competitors, local Chinese firms also actively absorb knowledge, which is demonstrated and leaked by foreign firms, to develop their unique technology (Ju et al. 2013). Therefore, innovation capabilities in Chinese firms, including Chinese subsidiaries and local firms, have been largely strengthened.

Domestically, in China's transitional economy, where ongoing institutional transitions are shaping the competition landscape, there are many uncertainties that firms need to buffer against and/or eliminate (Bao, Chen and Zhou 2012; Duanmu, Bu and Pittman 2018; Zhou and Li 2012). Undoubtedly, innovation is an effective strategy for local firms wishing to increase their domestic and international competitiveness and for China to survive amid global competition (Li and Atuahene-Gima 2001; Tellis, Prabhu, and Chandy 2009). Institutional and market environments both can influence the effectiveness of innovation in China (Gao et al. 2015).

However, in the context of China, this existing research lacks a clear recognition of how the institutional development, market complexity, internal business network, and external global network actively influence the innovation of domestic firms and foreign subsidiaries. Additionally, there is a gap in knowledge regarding the differences among innovation of local firms, subsidiaries, and MNCs and how they interact to create new knowledge through managing resources and networks worldwide. This omission simplifies the complexity of innovation in China, which is affected by both foreign MNCs and domestic firms.

Generally, this issue suggests that researchers should engage in closer examination of how the global networks contribute to innovation in China through international linkages and how domestic firms strengthen innovation capability with their own efforts. This issue aims to investigate innovation in China from both international linkages and indigenous effort. In doing so, we hope this issue enriches the literature on global network management and innovation in emerging economies with empirical studies employing a range of research methods: case study, secondary data, survey and fuzzy-set analysis.

The collection of articles published in this issue is classified into three categories according to aspects of their research topics. First, starting at the international level, two articles address the effects of Chinese-foreign linkages in innovation, either from the relationship perspective (Scott-Kennel, Yin, and Akoorie 2018) or the foreign ownership perspective (Yang and Wei 2018). Second, before moving to the domestic level, the moderating role of international linkages (e.g., global supply chain collaboration) is examined to understand the relationship between competition of unregistered firms and innovation of registered firms (Pérez et al. 2018). Third, at the domestic level, innovation is studied from both upstream and downstream of the value chain: consumers' decision-making in innovative products (Zhang, Hou, and Zhu 2018) and strategic choices, and environment constraints for product innovation (Ma and Jin 2018).

The first article, by Scott-Kennel, Yin, and Akoorie, titled "Innovation through Linkage, Leverage, and Learning: The Case of Monk Fruit Corporation," explores the role of Chinese-foreign linkages in the innovation trajectory of a Chinese firm. Adopting a widely used linkage, leverage, and learning (LLL) framework, the authors focus on innovation in the case firm and its partners through longitudinal analysis of archival case study data and interview data from key respondents. The developed framework extends the LLL framework by including the social networks and political context of China and linkages at individual, organizational, and institutional levels. The study finds that locally embedded linkages and foreign linkages contribute equally to firm's innovation. It also demonstrates that the firm's innovative and organizational development is inevitably intertwined with the process of learning, slowly achieved by leveraging linkages with both domestic and foreign partners. The study also concludes that the innovation collaboration has evolved from socially embedded to equity-based, over a long period of time.

The second article, by Yang and Wei, titled "Foreign Ownership and External Knowledge Acquisition: International Subsidiaries versus Local Firms in China," examines the relationship between foreign ownership and external knowledge acquisition in China and posits that international subsidiaries and local firms exhibit different rationales with regard to external knowledge acquisition. The study focuses on the effects of the global network on innovation in China, both for international subsidiaries and local firms. With a nationwide enterprise survey, the study concludes that foreign ownership positively affects external knowledge acquisition and that this relationship is moderated by both institutional legislation hazards and contract enforcement hazards. Interestingly, institutional legislation hazards have positive moderating effects, while contract enforcement hazards have negative moderating effects. The study contributes to knowledge about the role of foreign ownership in external knowledge acquisition in China and provides knowledge acquisition recommendations to the managers of international subsidiaries and local firms.

The third article, by Perez, Yang, Bai, Flores, and Heredia, titled "How Does Competition from Informal Firms Affect the Innovation of Formal Firms?", investigates how competition from informal firms affects the innovation of formal firms (informal firms, unlike formal firms, are firms that may not be registered and do operate outside of government regulation and taxation systems). By using survey data from Chinese manufacturing firms, the above authors find that informal firms' competition has a generally positive effect on the innovation of Chinese formal firms. However, the positive effect decreases when formal firms have high levels of supply chain collaborative capabilities. These findings provide two important managerial implications. First, formal firms must develop their organizational core competencies to face the challenges from informal ones; second, formal firms need to develop supply chain collaboration as a response strategy to sustain their competitive advantages.

The fourth article, by Zhang, Hou, and Zhu, titled "Applying Complexity Theory to Understand Chinese Consumers' Decision-making in Innovative Products," investigates consumers' behaviors in buying new products. In the presence of rapidly emerged new innovative products, how consumers select and buy their favorite products becomes important for product innovation. Using complexity theory, the authors identify the cognitive path of consumers in their decision-making: perceived risks (functional risk and emotional risk), innate innovativeness, and consumers' demographics related to information search (ongoing search and pre-purchase search). The study is among the first to apply a configurational analysis (i.e., qualitative comparative analysis [fQCA]) to explore paths in consumer decision-making in buying innovative products. The findings reveal that paths consist of perceived risks on information search from the configurations of consumer demographics and consumer innovativeness. These findings contribute to the literature regarding cognitive ways of consumer decision-making and innovation management, particularly in the context of China.

The fifth article, by Ma and Jin, titled "Success Factors for Product Innovation in China's Manufacturing Sector: Strategic Choice and Environment Constraints," explores the success factors for product innovation in China's manufacturing sector, based on an analysis of more than 700 enterprises. Rather than simply applying the theories of product innovation, often developed in the West, the authors take an indigenous perspective to examine the relationship between product innovation strategy, environment constraints, and firm performance as a result of aggregated product innovation activities, rather than focusing on a particular product innovation project. The findings reveal the important roles of product innovation strategy and environmental factors in helping improve firm performance at the organization level. In this way, Ma and Jin provide us a broader picture of product innovation and firm performance.

Collectively, the five articles of this issue highlight the difference of China's contextual environments as compared with the literature based on other countries. With the internationalization of Chinese firms and special attention to innovation in China, many questions are raised about the effects of international linkages with foreign MNCs and the indigenous efforts of domestic firms on firm innovation. This issue actively enters this conversation to investigate innovation in China at international and domestic levels. We believe that this issue makes an important attempt to extend existing knowledge on this subject and provides new insights to scholars and practitioners. We hope these articles will evoke further discussions and even debates on this important and interesting research area.

ACKNOWLEDGMENTS

Both Tian and Maoliang are very grateful for the help from Dr. Moshe Banai and Dr. Abraham Stefanidis towards this special issue.

FUNDING

Tian Wei acknoweldges the funding from National Natural Science Foundation of China (Grant No. 71772051), while Maoliang Bu acknowledges the funding from China' Ministry of Education)Grant No. 19YJA630002).

REFERENCES

Bao, Y., X. Chen, and K. Z. Zhou. 2012. "External Learning, Market Dynamics, and Radical Innovation: Evidence from China's High-Tech Firms." *Journal of Business Research* 65 (8):1226–33. doi: 10.1016/j.jbusres.2011.06.036.

Deng, P. 2003. "Foreign Direct Investment by Transnationals from Emerging Countries: The Case of China." *Journal of Leadership and Organizational Studies* 10 (2):113–24.

Duanmu, J., M. Bu, and R. Pittman. 2018. "Does Market Competition Dampen Environmental Performance? Evidence from China." *Strategic Management Journal* 39 (11):3006–30. doi: 10.1002/smj.2948.

Fan, P. 2006. "Catching up through Developing Innovation Capability: Evidence from China's Telecom-Equipment Industry." *Technovation* 26 (3):359–68. doi: 10.1016/j.technovation.2004.10.004.

Gao, Y., S. Gao, Y. Zhou, and K.-F. Huang. 2015. "Picturing Firms' Institutional Capital-Based Radical Innovation under China's Institutional Voids." *Journal of Business Research* 68 (6):1166–75. doi: 10.1016/j.jbusres.2014.11.011.

Ju, M., K. Z. Zhou, G. Y. Gao, and J. Lu. 2013. "Technological Capability Growth and Performance Outcome: Foreign versus Local Firms in China." *Journal of International Marketing* 21 (2):1–16. doi: 10.1509/jim.12.0171.

Li, H., and K. Atuahene-Gima. 2001. "Product Innovation Strategy and the Performance of New Technology Ventures in China." *Academy of Management Journal* 44 (6):1123–34.

Li, J., and J. Zhong. 2003. "Explaining the Growth of International R&D Alliances in China." *Managerial and Decision Economics* 24 (2–3):101–15. doi: 10.1002/mde.1079.

Pérez, J. A. H., S. Durst, M. H. Kunc, C. Geldes, and A. Flores. 2018. "Impact of Competition from Unregistered Firms on R&D Investment by Industrial Sectors in Emerging Economies." *Technological Forecasting and Social Change* 133 (4):179–89.

Tellis, G. J., J. C. Prabhu, and R. K. Chandy. 2009. "Radical Innovation across Nations: The Pre-Eminence of Corporate Culture." *Journal of Marketing* 73 (1):3–23. doi: 10.1509/jmkg.73.1.003.

Warner, M., N. S. Hong, and X. Xu. 2004. "Late Development Experience and the Evolution of Transnational Firms in the People's Republic Of China." *Asia Pacific Business Review* 10 (3–4):324–45. doi: 10.1080/1360238042000264397.

Zhang, Y. 2003. *China's Emerging Global Businesses: Political Economy and Institutional Investigations.* Basingstoke, UK: Palgrave Macmillan.

Zhou, K. Z., and C. B. Li. 2012. "How Knowledge Affects Radical Innovation: Knowledge Base, Market Knowledge Acquisition, and Internal Knowledge Sharing." *Strategic Management Journal* 33 (9):1090–102. doi: 10.1002/smj.1959.

Innovation Through Linkage, Leverage, and Learning: The Case of Monk Fruit Corporation

Joanna Scott-Kennel, Haolin Yin and Michele E. M. Akoorie

Abstract: This study investigates the role of Chinese-foreign linkages in the innovation trajectory of Guilin GFS Monk Fruit Corporation (Monk Fruit Corp.). Using the linkage-leverage-learning (LLL) framework as our starting point for analysis and integrating complementary theory, we build a relationally and contextually oriented framework for assessing innovation. Longitudinal analysis of archival data, and insights from key respondents, demonstrates that the firm's innovative and organizational development is inextricably entwined with the process of learning, achieved overtime by leveraging linkages with both domestic and foreign partners. The results also reveal how independent research and development (R&D), coupled with skill in relationship building, applied by the Chinese firm and the individuals within it, can provide an equally important support structure to Sino-foreign innovation. Our results reaffirm the importance of collaboration, but also demonstrate its limits as collaborative organizational relationships evolve from being socially to equity-based over time.

INTRODUCTION

Linkages between local and foreign organizations and the professionals that work within them enable firms to leverage capacity, obtain external resources, learn new knowledge, and consequently, enhance R&D efficiency by alleviating risks and costs (Hagedoorn and Schakenraad 1994; Ahuja 2000; Stuart 2000; Giroud and Scott-Kennel 2009; Fan 2014). Such relationships can be a critical source of knowledge to fuel corporate innovation (Cantwell 2017), particularly for enterprises in emerging economies, such as China, that have been characterized as having fewer advantages relative to international competitors (Sun and Zhou 2011; Fan 2014). Innovation in emerging economies is on the rise, and China's science and technology development plan (2006–2020) recognizes enterprises as the principal force driving this innovation through collaboration (Chadee, Sharma, and Roxas 2017).

Focus by the extant literature on the role of the foreign multinational enterprise (MNE) in Sino-foreign joint ventures tends to obscure the interdependent role played by local individuals, organizations, and institutions. Nor are there many studies that consider the impact on focal firm innovation via both domestic and international linkages with both national and foreign firms. This leaves a considerable gap in our understanding of how such relationships evolve over time. To address this issue, this study includes a broad range of linkages, both at home and abroad.

The aim of this study is to investigate how Chinese firms facilitate innovation via linkages. We apply Mathews' (2006a) linkage, leverage, and linkage (LLL) framework of emerging or "dragon" multinational internationalization to relationships formed by Chinese multinational, Guilin GFS Monk Fruit Corporation (Monk Fruit Corp.). This firm was selected because its collaborative innovation has gone hand in hand with international/organizational growth and change. The LLL framework explains how latecomers and newcomers can leverage resources via linkages to compete rather than just "catch up" with incumbents in a networked global economy, making it an ideal framework to address the topic of innovation through LLL.

This empirical investigation of emerging multinational innovation, and its approach and scope viewed through the LLL lens, extends Mathews' framework by inclusion of China's unique social networks and political context, and linkages at individual, organizational, and institutional levels (Meyer 2007; Voss, Buckley and Cross 2010). We look at innovation by the firm and its partners, and find that locally-based linkages contribute as much to innovation as linkages with foreign partners. Our results demonstrate that, over the course of its development, the complexity of the firm's linkage network history has not only facilitated product and process innovation, but also changed the nature of the organization from one based on relational ties and social capital to formal ties based on ownership (equity investment), where the local partner first learns from and then overtakes its erstwhile foreign partner.

The article is organized as follows. First, we develop a conceptual framework that builds on the LLL framework, emphasizing the institutional context by drawing on complementary theory and empirical evidence. Second, we briefly outline the research methods and company/industry profile. Third, we present our findings with specific emphasis on innovation through LLL, and how individual, organizational, and institutional relationships change over time. Last, we present the discussion, propositions and a model, then conclusions.

LITERATURE

Linkage, Leverage and Learning (LLL)

Mathews' (2002a, 2006a) LLL framework asserts that innovative firms from emerging markets, the so-called "dragon multinationals," leverage their international connections to overcome a shortage of resources at home (Mathews 2006a; Luo and Wang 2012; Tiwari, Sen and Shaik 2016). The focus of the literature on horizontal linkages (Gulati, Nohria and Zaheer 2000; Liu and Buck 2009; Li et al. 2016) suggests they are preferred by MNEs from emerging economies, as the means, through collaborative activity, to access foreign markets, assets, and resources (Wang 2002), and to assimilate organizational capabilities and knowledge. Leverage of such linkages occurs through imitation, transfer, or substitution of resources of partner firms, and learning occurs during the process of repeating linkage and leverage (Mathews 2002b, 2006a, Yeganeh 2016; Chadee, Sharma, and Roxas 2017).

Emphasis on resources by the LLL framework aligns to organizational and strategic innovation by Chinese firms. The link between resources and innovation lies in the fact that the liabilities of lateness (Mathews 2002a, 2006a; Li 2007; Luo and Wang 2012), newness, foreignness, and country of origin (Thite, Wilkinson, Budhwar and Mathews 2016; Tiwari, Sen and Shaik 2016) faced by emerging MNEs relate to poor branding and marketing infrastructure, insufficient knowledge-related resources and capabilities, and lack of advanced technology (Tiwari, Sen and Shaik 2016). In contrast to developed country MNEs, which have unique firm- or ownership-specific advantages prior to internationalization, as per Dunning's (2000), Ownership-Location-Internationalization (OLI) paradigm, emerging MNEs are more likely to seek such advantages through international acquisition (Rui and Yip 2008).

As the LLL framework takes as its basis the resource-based view (RBV) of the firm (Barney 1991; Penrose 1959), we can argue that the global expansion of newcomer MNEs from emerging economies is motivated by resource linkage and learning (Peng 2001; Mathews 2006a), new competences (Boisot and Meyer 2008), advanced technology, and strategic expertise (Rugman and Li 2007). This is why latecomer firms also tend to rely on partnerships and joint ventures for such resources, to reduce the high level of risk involved with more leveraged strategies. The contribution of Mathews' (2006a) framework is to demonstrate how a firm uses linkages and learning to leverage these resources across national boundaries. However, as Kellermans et al. (2016) point out, resources are not always well-defined, often inconsistent, and yield contradictory results across studies.

We sharpen our understanding of the nature of such resources by focusing specifically on innovation rather than internationalization. We also broaden our view of the source and location of such resources. In contrast to Mathews' work, and much that has followed that emphasizes the relationship between LLL and outward internationalization, we argue for inward oriented leverage achieved via joint collaboration with domestic firms at home, with foreign affiliates based locally, as well as with foreign partners based overseas (Lu et al. 2017). This inward/outward looking approach is also supported by work on Sino-foreign joint ventures and international alliances (Hagedoorn and Schakenraad 1994; Stuart 2000), which demonstrates upgrading both at home and abroad, and by work on foreign-local linkages that suggests local firms in transitional economies benefit from foreign innovation via inward foreign direct investment (Jindra, Giroud and Scott-Kennel 2009). Thus, the source and location of resources can be foreign or local.

Further, the institutional context needs greater empirical attention with regard to innovation by latecomer firms (Yeganeh 2016). Huang and Tsang (2016) add the institutional dimension to their LLL-based analysis of Acer's internationalization, explicitly recognizing the importance of cultural, political, and technological contexts to the growth of latecomer emerging market multinationals. The authors argue that institutions matter, and that the LLL model neglects the interdependence of institutions (including networks both at home and abroad) and strategies, and the subsequent effects on innovation. We concur with Huang and Tseng, and suggest that in addition to innovation (i.e., technological context), there are two missing links in Mathews' (2006a) explanation of the emerging MNE. The first is an institutions-based view of latecomer innovation, and in particular social capital embodied in linkages and networks as explanation of how relationships between MNEs and foreign partners are created (Narula 2006). The second omission, and this applies particularly to emerging MNEs from China, is that the rise of the "dragon" multinational has a political dimension, which fits with Meyer's (2007) view of the importance of institutional context. These are discussed in the following section.

Social Capital, Networks, and Political Context of Latecomer Firms

The concept of social capital, defined by Fukuyama as "a country's stock of informal values or norms shared among members of a group that permits cooperation between them" (Fukuyama 1999, 16), provides the theoretical foundation for social and business networks. The importance of business ties in the Chinese cultural context cannot be overstated, and social capital is built on connections based on trust. Reciprocal relationships with business partners can counteract the low level of trust found in collectivist nations such as China (Bjorkman and Kock 1995; Fukuyama 1999; Rao, Pearce and Xin 2005; Huff and Kelley 2003). Guanxi relationships, where one person has a "tie" or "connection" to another person (Gao, Knight and Ballantyne 2012), can help mitigate risks, encourage reciprocation, and begin the process of developing trust.

Dunning identified relational assets as "the accumulated societal fund of economic relationships, which are embodied or re-posited in both individuals, organizations, and networks of organizations, engaging in economic activity" (2003, 12), shifting focus away from the view that income generating assets are purely physical and financial. Dunning does not specifically mention *guanxi* in this contribution, but his list of relational virtues/values include reciprocity, trust and loyalty and the functions which they inform, such as innovation, production, and subcontracting, reveal marked similarities to *guanxi*. Therefore, we use the notion of relational assets in our conceptual framework (Figure 1), with the subscript *guanxi* and explain how relational assets are linked with LLL and OLI and can manifest at individual, organizational and institutional levels.

Emerging market multinationals characterize both government and private capital (and influence) (Accenture 2008). In the case of China, outflow of foreign direct investment (FDI) from the early 1980s was motivated by the need for natural resources, capital, technology, and information, and is strictly controlled—and encouraged through incentives—by government (Aggarwal and Agmon 1990; Mathews 2002a), creating a politico-economic link that is quite different from government intervention in developed countries. One could also argue that the promotion of MNEs in the context of China is in accord with national strategy—that is, to strengthen China's competitiveness in the international arena (Mingjiang 2008). Just as the postwar Western (principally American) MNEs brought with them the notion of

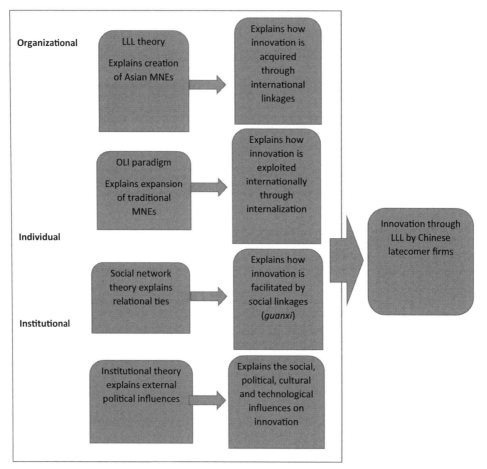

FIGURE 1. Conceptual Framework

westernized culture, consumerism, and technology, so too could nascent Chinese MNEs be demonstrating China's socioeconomic success in providing an alternative internationalization model, aimed at boosting China's influence in the world.

 The link between relational assets and political influence is clear if we understand that international cooperation for Chinese firms provides a valuable opportunity for the expression of "harmony" that underpins Chinese culture. Further, given the relatively weak regulatory and institutional environments at home, international activities undertaken by emerging MNEs tend to be supported by social networks, and innovative activities tend to rely more heavily on existing or modified technologies, originally developed in more advanced economies (Cuervo-Cazurra and Genc 2008; Gammeltoft, Barnard and Madhok 2010). Leveraging linkages internationally for innovation, therefore, is heavily dependent on the strength of relationships between individuals as well as those formed with government and industry.

Figure 1 shows the conceptual framework that we have developed from our discussion of the literature. On the left are the extant theoretical explanations for the MNE: the LLL framework focused on "latecomer" MNEs, and the OLI paradigm focused on developed country MNEs, which are complementary, as both types of MNE seek resources and assets through mergers and acquisitions (M&As) and cross-border inter-organizational linkages. The last two boxes on the left extend these models to include institutional dimensions and informal relational assets (social capital), the more formal political influence of government encouraging outward FDI, and social linkages encouraging collaborative organizational forms.

Our framework extends the extant literature on several other dimensions; explicit inclusion of linkages at multiple levels of analysis (individual, organizational, and institutional), and implicit inclusion (via our research method, below) of different types of linkages that involve no, partial, or full ownership, as well as those formed with both at local and foreign partners. The remainder of this article seeks to explore these linkages with regard to innovation, focusing on leverage of resources for innovation via these linkages and subsequent organizational learning at Monk Fruit Corp.

METHODS

The illustrative case of Monk Fruit Corp. was selected on the basis of its relevance to our understanding of LLL and innovation by latecomer multinationals. It is important to recognize that it is the interaction between linkages and leverage that leads to learning, and that this is a path-dependent process that can only be evaluated by looking at linkages and their subsequent impacts over time. So, in order to investigate this phenomenon, we adopted a longitudinal approach using a single in-depth case study. This approach enables us to make use of triangulation within data and theories to consider both the phenomenon (LLL) and the institutional context (social and political influences on emerging Chinese multinationals) interdependently (Yin 2014; Eisenhardt and Graebner 2007). It also reveals the interplay between dynamic constructs (Siggelkow 2007), enabling us to define data points, and specific incidents occurring at points in time, enabling us to draw inferences from the data.

In essence, our approach to data collection was centered on the strategy of bricolage—which is based on using a diverse range of resources—and triangulation (Jick 1979). This study made use of multiple sources of data for the firm, including interviews, insights, communication and clarification from company informants, visits to the sites in New Zealand and China, and secondary/archival sources: company annual reports, newsletters, prior published case studies, magazines, and other information from the firm's websites, including press releases. Overall, we created a fairly comprehensive set of data from which we identified key themes around the process of leveraging linkages for learning and innovation.

The qualitative research design involved pre-conceptualization of issues developed from the literature review (Miles and Huberman 1994) or "*a priori* categorization" (Sinkovics, Penz, and Ghauri 2008). Descriptive and subsequent pattern matching was applied in the process of the data analysis to enable us to develop insights into the major emergent themes and dimensions, and also their dynamic interrelationships (Gioia, Corley, and Hamilton 2013).

Looking back, and then forward, with regard to innovation development, revealed further archival material, such as radio interviews and television documentaries on the company and its founders. Patent applications (for the process of extraction of mogroside sweetener for use in food products), self-notified applications for mogroside to be accepted as "generally regarded as safe" (GRAS) by the United States (U.S.) Food and Drug Administration (FDA), also provided valuable insights into the detailed scientific evidence required before this could be sold as a "natural sweetener."

Having assembled this dossier of evidence, each of the authors examined the material independently and then discussed the findings in order to reach consensual decisions on all the major emergent concepts, themes, and analysis on dynamic interrelationships. We were then able to interview a key respondent, Mr. Fusheng Lan (CEO, Director, and Legal representative of Monk Fruit Corp., co-founder of the Guilin GFS Bio-Tech joint venture, and founder/Director of Guilin Bio-DaDi) in September 2016. In order to facilitate recall and avoid personal opinion that may have compromised validity of responses through reluctance to answer, we confined our questions to the specific innovative processes that had involved the focal firm independently or with foreign firms/individuals, Chinese partners, and professionals from China and overseas. Mr. Lan was not only willing to answer our questions but frequently checked the data we had collected via email and text communications and provided more information on all R&D and innovations associated with linkages between these firms and partners as the study progressed (July 9, 2017; October 9, 2017; November 27, 2017). Observations were also made during visits to BioVittoria's operations in New Zealand (September 2016), and later, Guilin GFS Monk Fruit Corp. in China (November 2017).

Rather than adopt a procedural approach to data interpretation, we followed the suggestion of Gioia, Corley, and Hamilton (2013) that the benefits of qualitative research are its flexibility in applying different approaches to fit different phenomenological needs. Therefore, we took an innovative approach to new concept development and application through abductive reasoning. Since abduction depends on mental processes that are not necessarily conscious and deliberate, its explanatory hypotheses should be optimally simple and should have consequences with a conceivable practical bearing that allow at least mental tests (Dubois and Gadde 2002). By adopting this approach, we took what may be seen as an incomplete set of observations and proceed to the likeliest possible explanation. In other words, abductive reasoning enables reviewing of relationships among the emergent concepts that explain the phenomenon of interest and clarifies relevant data-to-theory connections (Gioia, Corley, and Hamilton 2013).

In order to address the primary research question, namely how Chinese firms facilitate innovation through international linkages, we first focused on the development of the relationship between Guilin GFS Bio-Tech and BioVittoria (the precursor companies to Monk Fruit Corp.) and then on other linkages throughout Monk Fruit Corp.'s life-cycle, from its Chinese origins in monk fruit growing through its process of internationalization and absorption of Guilin Bio-DaDi and BioVittoria. Our preliminary analysis (see Appendix A) categorized data by linkage between individuals, organizations, and institutions. The resources leveraged in each of these relationships were identified, as was the learning in the form of specific innovations. Returning to Mathews' (2006a) LLL article, his mention of strategic and organizational innovation, in conjunction with further review of the changing structure of the organization around financing and ownership, prompted analysis beyond the product/ process and market related innovation we were seeing in the preliminary results, and a shift in focus towards what can be viewed as structural innovations by the firm. This provided the basis for the second part of the discussion of our results. First, we present a company and industry profile.

MONK FRUIT CORPORATION

In 2001, Mr. Fusheng Lan, China's leading scientific expert on monk fruit "established Guilin Bio-DaDi [supplier of monk fruit tissue culture and seedlings] as an independent legal entity" (Lan, personal communication, October 9, 2017). In 2003, BioVittoria (New Zealand) was established to further Dr. Garth Smith's work on the monk fruit sweetener extraction method. Dr. Lan and Dr. Smith formalized their existing relationship in May 2004 with the formation of Guilin GFS Bio-Tech Co., a joint venture between Dr. Lan and BioVittoria. In 2014, BioVittoria's assets were transferred to the Guilin GFS Bio-Tech joint venture and incorporated, along with Guilin Bio-DaDi Co. Ltd., into Monk Fruit Corp. (est. 2015). Monk Fruit Corp. occupied a niche "in an advanced ingredient supply chain by providing the global food and beverage industry with monk fruit-based sweeteners, juice concentrate, dry fruit and tea" (Monk Fruit Corp 2017). The company had "70% international market share" (Feng 2015), and controlled over 60% of the monk fruit crop and over 90% of monk fruit-based ingredient production and sales worldwide (Osborne and Benson-Rea 2014).

Monk Fruit Corp. operates in the rapidly growing global market of natural high intensive sweeteners (HIS), which was forecast to be worth US$1.7 billion in 2017, and to grow to US$2 billion by 2022 (PRNewswire 2017). Although the natural sugar market is still much larger than both the artificial and natural sweetener markets combined, consumer demand for natural sugar substitutes is growing, driven by health concerns over rising levels of obesity and poor dental health in developed country markets. The challenge for food producers, including Monk Fruit Corp., is "ensuring such sweeteners meet FDA approval requirements, as well as consumer expectations" (Lan, personal communication, September, 13, 2016) for good health and taste within cost and performance parameters. The onus is on manufacturers to offer scientific proof that food additives do not have carcinogenic properties before they can be included in the GRAS notification program.

Stevia extract, derived from the leaves of the stevia plant native to South America, has been the primary beneficiary of consumer interest in natural sweeteners, followed by monk fruit extract. For the past 800 years, monk fruit (*Luo Han Guo*), a small melon, has been grown in its native region of Guilin, Guangxi Province, China, where 90 percent of monk fruit production takes place. There is a government-imposed monopoly on the cultivation of monk fruit. It is illegal to grow this plant outside of China, and in 2004 the Chinese government forbade the export of seeds or seedlings of monk fruit. Chinese agro-business has been promoted by the Chinese government (www.chinaag.org) and the promise of returns has attracted other players, such as Guilin Layn Natural Ingredients (www.layncorp.com) and

GLG Life Tech Corporation (led by Canadian Chinese CEO, Luke Zhang, www.glglifetech. com), who have trade-marked their own monk fruit products and are building processing capacity in Guilin. However, unlike Monk Fruit Corp. they have also diversified their natural HIS interests to include stevia. China's production of stevia accounts for around 80 per cent of the world supply.

Linkages, Leverage, and Learning at Monk Fruit Corp.

We present our initial findings relating to the case in the table in Appendix A, specifically individual (personal), organizational (firm), and institutional (government, industry) linkages formed under the broader Monk Fruit Corp. umbrella that enabled leverage of resources for innovation and organizational learning. These are discussed below.

BioVittoria and the Guilin GFS Bio-Tech Joint Venture

BioVittoria was established in 2003 in Hamilton, New Zealand, by HortResearch scientist, Dr. Garth Smith, Dr. Andrew Rubman, and Mr. Stephen LeFebvre. Mr. Fusheng Lan and Dr. Smith developed a method of extracting sweetener from monk fruit that was 300 times sweeter than cane sugar (branded as PureLo: natural calorie free sweetener). BioVittoria established an overseas office in the United States, which functioned as a sales and marketing arm for local markets (Osborne and Benson-Rea 2014).

The linkage between BioVittoria and monk fruit development work in China was centered on the science-based social connection between Smith and Lan. As early as 1987, Smith was employed by the Guangxi Institute of Botany of the Chinese Academy of Sciences as a foreign expert. By 2002, Lan faced "a 'bottleneck' in the development of extraction technology of Luo Han Guo sweet glycosides" (Chen 2008), and hence sought to collaborate with Smith. Then, in 2004, Smith "retired from HortResearch in New Zealand and moved to Guilin in 2006" (Lan, personal communication, November 28, 2017).

This linkage at the individual level was formalized at the organizational level through the "formation of Guilin GFS Bio-Tech, a 50/50 joint venture co-founded by Lan and BioVittoria" (personal communication, Lan, October 9, 2017), which served to deepen the professional relationship between Smith and Lan. Guilin GFS Bio-Tech was responsible for sourcing monk fruit, producing sweetener and providing the base for R&D (laboratories) for BioVittoria in China, while BioVittoria specialized in undertaking R&D relating to the sweetener, final product marketing and sales (observation Monk Fruit Corp. visit, November 7, 2017).

This joint venture enabled better leverage of capabilities embodied in the founders than if they had continued to operate more independently, as both offered complementary skills and linkages to the venture. Lan's expertise in monk fruit cultivation developed through working as Vice-Director (Monk Fruit Corp 2015a) for government-owned Guangxi Institute of Botany of the Chinese Academy of Sciences, and as head of Guilin Bio-DaDi. Further, strong and stable relationships with local government (as a member of the Guilin Municipal Committee and supervisor of Guilin Lijiang Rural Cooperative Bank) facilitated access to governmental and financial support. Local connections (e.g., Vice Chairman of the Guangxi Association of Overseas and Returned Scholars, Vice Chairman of the Guilin Plant Extraction Association, and Chairman of Guilin Monk Fruit Association) (Monk Fruit Corp 2015a) facilitated access to human capital and promoted inter-industry learning and development.

Garth Smith was also recognized worldwide for his expertise in horticultural and botanical product development in the food industry. When working as a scientist at Crown Research Institute HortResearch, Smith was involved in varietal development, new canopy management, and cropping techniques, and was considered to be "one of the pioneering figures of the New Zealand kiwifruit industry in 1980s and 1990s" (Osborne and Benson-Rea 2014, 2). His experience coupled with the R&D base at Guilin GFS Bio-Tech in China enabled Smith to develop a method of extracting sweetener (Mogroside) from monk fruit. As Smith explained in a 2010 television documentary on *Luo Han Guo* "the sweetness is tied up in a complex molecule—so it tastes sweet on the tongue, but the human digestive system can't absorb it" (National Bank Country Calendar 2010). Along with his marketing and sales team at BioVittoria, Smith successfully launched this innovative product globally. His scientific experience was invaluable in filing successful patent applications for the extraction process (www.google.com/patents/WO2008030121A1?cl=en) and, later, for the juice extraction process and for self-determined GRAS applications, which required detail on lengthy and intensive scientific procedures.

Leverage of the R&D capabilities and financial resources supplied by both joint venture partners has led to innovation relating to cultivation, planting, and products. Table 1 provides a chronological summary of the innovations and intellectual property created by the firms that would later form the Monk Fruit Corp. Group (BioVittoria in New Zealand, and the Guilin GFS Bio-Tech Joint Venture and Guilin DaDi in China) and the source of these innovations. Table 1 shows 18 innovations derived from these focal firms' own R&D activities; ten involved foreign professionals; another three developed innovation from partner firms. Although the table attributes just one innovation to a foreign firm, this does not account for BioVittoria's involvement in nine other innovations, nor does it include the international marketing relationships with foreign firms (see Appendix A). In sum, Monk Fruit's growth has relied on mastering core technologies through their own R&D along with that of partners and foreign professionals. This approach would later bring them negotiation power when leveraging financial resources of potential investors.

Leverage of Industry Linkages in China

The ability for ongoing collaboration and innovation, in large part, is a result of strong regional linkages characterizing the monk fruit industry in Guilin. In 2006, the Fruit-Sweetness Monk Fruit Association was established and since then has supported farmers in more than "150 villages in 9 counties to plant more than 7,000 hectares of monk fruit orchards" and by 2015 Monk Fruit Corp. had "6,000 monk fruit farmers" based around Guilin (Feng 2015). These domestic linkages took precedence in the early years, and provided a supportive framework for developments at Guilin GFS Bio-Tech and later at Monk Fruit Corp.

TABLE 1
Innovation and Intellectual Property at Monk Fruit Corp., by Source and Focal Firm

Year	Innovation	Source	Focal firm
2001	Developed tip meristem virus-free culture and rapid multiplication of monk fruit[b]	4	GDD
2002	Invented and commercialized tissue culture technology for monk fruit seedlings[a]	4	GBTJV
	Registered plant variety rights for new superior varieties of monk fruit[a]	4	GBTJV
2004~	GFS development and operation model - "enterprise + orchard + specialized cooperative + grower" industrial chain[b]	4	GBTJV
2006	Rapid manufacturing technology for high purity monk fruit glycosides[b]	2	GBTJV, BV
2007~	Invented and commercialized a technique for making monk fruit extract with at least 40% purity (the content of mogroside V)[a]	2	GBTJV, BV
2008	Monk fruit controlled atmosphere cold storage technology[b]	2	GBTJV, BV
	Extraction technology of monk fruit mogroside (IP)[b]	2	GBTJV, BV
2008~	Developed technology for large-scale cultivation and production of monk fruit[b]	4	GDD
2009	Developed large scale monk fruit orchards[a]	4	GBTJV
	Pioneered the use of environmentally-friendly orchard technology such as drip irrigation for reducing water and fertilizer usage[a]	4	GBTJV
2010	Guilin GFS Bio-Tech attained US FDA-GRAS approval (Jan.)[a]	2	GBTJV, BV
	Developed monk fruit standardized cultivation technique[b]	4	GDD
2012	Developed monk fruit standardized cultivation technique[b]	4	GBTJV
2012~	Invented a process for making a clean tasting, stable monk fruit juice[a]	2	GBTJV, BV
2013	Deionized monk fruit concentrate production technology[a,b]	2	GBTJV, BV
	Monk fruit by-products secondary production technology[b]	2	GBTJV, BV
	Patent for extraction technology of monk fruit mogroside (IP)[b]	2	GBTJV, BV
	Develop technology for spray pollination of monk fruit[b]	3	GDD
2014	Developed information management system for monk fruit standardized cultivation[a,b]	4	GBTJV
	Developed and commercialized technology for spray pollination of monk fruit[a,b]	4	GBTJV
	Developed technique of removing pesticide residues in monk fruit powder[b]	4	GBTJV
	Developed and commercialized nutrient solution and method of application for spray pollination of monk fruit (IP)[b]	4	GBTJV
	Developed integrated water-fertilizer-drug irrigation technique of monk fruit[b]	4	GDD
2015	Developed comprehensive utilization technique for by-products of monk fruit sweet glycosides by column[b]	4	MFC
	Developed an information administration system of monk fruit material recall[b]	4	MFC
	Patent for monk fruit extract and extraction method (IP)[b]	2	MFC GDD
	Monk fruit multi-storied culture technique[b]	3	
2016	Developed monk fruit concentrate (glycoside free or low glycoside)[b]	4	MFC
	Developed monk fruit tea cream production technique[b]	4	MFC
	The monk fruit extract attained US FDA-GRAS approval as a sweetener including the usage for baby food (Sept.)[a]	1	MFC

BV: BioVittoria; GBTJV: Guilin GFS Bio-Tech joint venture; GDD: Guilin Bio-DaDi; MFC: Monk Fruit Corp.

1 = Involvement of foreign firm; 2 = Involvement of foreign professional; 3 = Attained from partner firm; 4 = Focal firm's own R&D activity.

[a]Information sourced from Monk Fruit Corp 2015c;

[a]From Fusheng Lan 2017.

The ability to leverage linkages with local growers and the Monk Fruit Association facilitated operations and encouraged innovation in a vertically integrated value chain. Monk Fruit Corp. claims to be "the only [monk fruit] company in the world with in-house capability for the entire supply chain . . . from seedling to finished product" (Monk Fruit Corp 2015b), including in-house expertise spanning monk fruit genetic resources, superior plant varieties, seedling cultivation technology and capability, farmer training, orchard technology research and development, monk fruit processing for extract and juice products, and selling and marketing of monk fruit ingredients (Monk Fruit Corp 2015b).

In 2013, linkage with the tissue culture seedling production center of Guilin Bio-DaDi further strengthened the "company's ability to innovate by [leveraging its] partners' local ingenuity, experience and connections with international partners" (Lan, personal communication, September 13, 2016) (see Table 1, for innovation undertaken at Guilin Bio-DaDi by source).

Leverage of International Linkages

Linkages with other organizations also contributed to the company's financial resources, initially through BioVittoria's connections in New Zealand.

> In 2008 there was a second stage of investment ... [into Monk Fruit Corp. from New Zealand investors including] the New Zealand Government. These funds were used ... to complete the first ever purpose-built monk fruit processing facility, near Guilin. The company owns 26,000 m^3 of refrigerated storage and 8,000 m^2 of plant and has processing capacity for over 30,000 tons of fresh monk fruit and a tissue culture seedling production center with an annual output of 4 million seedlings. (Monk Fruit Corp 2015a)

International linkages (pre-dating the Guilin GFS Bio-Tech joint venture) were also paramount to successful marketing and distribution of monk fruit products. David Thorrold, who joined BioVittoria as CEO in 2006, had already developed "an extensive network of contacts in the U.S. and European food and beverage industries" (Monk Fruit Corp 2015b) and spearheaded the global launch of BioVittoria's "Fruit-Sweetness" product (observation during the second authors' visit to BioVittoria, September 22, 2016). With GRAS notification being achieved in 2010, the company could integrate their extract into the products of food and beverage companies worldwide, including as follows:

> Nestlé, Pepsico, The Coca-Cola Company, Uni-President, General Mills, Kellogg and Chobani [and] . . . in the U.S. Natural soda maker Zevia, ice cream maker Arctic Zero, juice company Califia Farms, baked goods brand Vitalicious and So Delicious Dairy Free are just a few of the up-and-coming brands that have developed products with monk fruit. (Monk Fruit Corp 2015a)

These linkages would lead to more lucrative contracts for the firm, including the exclusive strategic partnership formed with one of the world's largest ingredient companies, British sugar firm Tate & Lyle (2010–2015):

> Tate & Lyle today announced it has entered into a five-year strategic partnership agreement with BioVittoria Ltd. for the exclusive global marketing and distribution rights for BioVittoria's

monk fruit. Tate & Lyle will be marketing the products in the U.S. under the PUREFRUIT(TM) brand name. (Anonymous 2011)

The partnership not only contributed to innovation diffusion but also helped the company become an ingredient supplier for McNeil Nutritionals and increased its credibility internationally. As Thorrold explains, "Through our partnership with Tate & Lyle we have been able to offer McNeil great ingredient innovation, backed by our unique, world-class monk fruit supply chain" (Professional Services 2012).

Linkages such as these also enabled Guilin GFS Bio-Tech to "establish its brands ahead of competitors'" (Lan, personal communication, November 7, 2017) and competing products, such as those sweetened with natural stevia extract. Calorie free natural sweetener NECTRESSE™, Fruit Sweetness, and PureLo were making inroads in international markets via such linkages, and in 2015, Sweet-Delicious (a low-calorie natural sweetener) was launched internationally. Protecting innovation remained important to leveraging the company's cache of innovatory capabilities internationally. Guilin Bio-Tech and its partners have obtained plant variety rights on different varieties of seedlings, patents, production process; trademarked its brands and; secured co-exclusive use of a patent formerly owned by Procter & Gamble (Osborne and Benson-Rea, 2014).

Organizational Learning through Linkages

Learning, over time, is evident in the linkage and leverage trajectory of Monk Fruit Corp., though it is not only limited to specific innovation (see Table 1). It is also demonstrated by the company's progression from individual to organizational level relationships; technologically-based relationships between scientists to inter-firm relationships involving agreements for supply, marking, and distribution; and a shift in emphasis from domestic linkages with local growers, industry associations, and government support (direct and indirect) to include application and exploitation of the dynamic core capabilities of key personnel and their contacts in the international realm.

We find individual connections and expertise crucial in the early stages of organizational learning. For instance, Lan's rich experience of study, research, and work overseas broadened his horizons and enabled him to establish linkages to foreign resources including capital, technology, techniques and experts (Osborne and Benson-Rea 2014). Leverage of such linkages has played an important role in learning, influencing decision-making, and implementation of strategies with regard to innovation and the development of the monk fruit business.

Organizational learning in a strategic sense is also apparent as the company's external business network broadens, internal structures are streamlined through M&A and internationalization of the company progresses. This has been achieved, primarily, by cementing key linkages through equity investment (e.g., the Guilin GFS Bio-Tech joint venture between Lan and BioVittoria, then the purchase and integration of BioVittoria and seedling company, Guilin DaDi into Guilin GFS Monk Fruit Corp). The establishment of Guilin GFS Bio-Tech and later Monk Fruit Corp. facilitated control over a greater number of cross-border linkages as organizational connections replaced individual connections.

Collaboration with foreign experts has helped created dozens of innovations including new techniques and patents, and has earned approval for product innovations into overseas market entries. Furthermore, the marketing experience of sales professionals based in New Zealand and connections made through the U.S. branches of foreign partner BioVittoria contributed to market-led innovation in the China's headquarters and greater international presence (Osborne and Benson-Rea 2014, 4). It is also instructive to note that relationships that were further from home and non-core to the company's competitiveness (e.g., international market linkages, such as Tate & Lyle), remained as collaborative rather than equity-based linkages.

Organizational Innovation

In 2009, BioVittoria attempted to attract public investment by launching an IPO for NZ$20 million. However, the IPO failed to reach the minimum subscription level of NZ$8 million and was withdrawn. Two years later, BioVittoria turned to Tate & Lyle, entering into a five-year strategic partnership for a 12 percent equity stake: "As time went on BioVittoria got further into financial difficulties and by 2014 the company was in a precarious state as a result of rising fruit prices and the high cost of production" (Bridgeman 2015, 8). In August 2014, a special meeting of shareholders was held to vote on a transaction which would pass majority ownership of BioVittoria to new Chinese investors. BioVittoria was acquired through Guilin GFS Bio-Tech, and along with the recently acquired Guilin Bio-DaDi, these three firms were then restructured into the Guilin GFS Monk Fruit Corporation (Monk Fruit Corp.). The Chinese investors achieved a majority shareholding (77%) in Monk Fruit Corp. paying the price of eight cents per share, valuing the BioVittoria shares at NZ$3.7 million:

> Intellectual Property rights were sold to Guilin Bio-Tech and debt owed to Tate & Lyle (NZ$2.5 million) would be repaid from the proceeds. Inter-company debt owed to Guilin Bio-Tech would be repaid over the two-year duration of a new Tate & Lyle contract, which provided the company with a fixed margin on product sold. (Bridgeman 2015, 8)

The outcome of this reorganization was that BioVittoria, once 86 percent owned by New Zealand interests, was now owned by Chinese investors, who then completed a new round of equity funding, re-branded the company as Monk Fruit Corp., increased the grower network and doubled the fruit supply. As a co-founder of BioVittoria, Stephen Lefebvre commented that from a local perspective, "It's a travesty what happened to [BioVittoria] . . . [the takeover is] not a good situation for New Zealand, the shareholders and for business people in general" (cited in Bridgeman 2015, 8). Yet, not all local operations were lost:

> BioVittoria was re-structured to become the New Zealand subsidiary of the company, responsible for developing and managing local New Zealand and Asia Pacific markets, and the American office of BioVittoria in Chicago was re-structured as Guilin GFS' U.S. branch responsible for sales and marketing in the Americas. (Monk Fruit Corp 2015a).

Ironically, the Chinese co-founder of the original joint venture, Lan, became CEO and a Director of Monk Fruit Corp, while one of the original BioVittoria team and CEO since

2006, David Thorrold, became Vice President and General Manager, Sales and Marketing. Smith was no longer involved. The largest shareholder and President was Simon Chuang, who according to the company's website has "deep expertise in consulting in the motor vehicle, household appliance, catering, pharmaceutical, medical, industrial products and food industries" (Monk Fruit Corp 2017).

DISCUSSION AND PROPOSITIONS

In line with the extant literature on innovation and capability building, we find innovation by an emerging MNE strongly associated with the collaborative interplay between individuals, organizations, and institutions. We can derive three important theoretical insights from our analysis of the case. The first relates to the location and nature of linkages and leverage of resources for innovation. Mathews proposed that "a global orientation becomes a source of advantage—since the opportunities through which it can expand are likely to be found in the global market rather than in its domestic environment" (2006a, 18). However, our focus on innovation rather than internationalization suggests some qualification of this argument. Although LLL emphasizes access to technology and "leapfrogging" into global markets in order to compete with incumbents in developed economies, Monk Fruit Corp., unlike other examples of latecomer multinationals, does not achieve this through purchase of assets in a developed country using outward FDI (e.g., Lenovo (IBM), see Liu and Buck 2009). Monk Fruit Corp.'s innovation trajectory is initially characterized by collaboration between individuals in the Chinese context, and their personal links to local institutions and firms locally. Then the innovation-related resources of foreign partner BioVittoria are, for the most part, relocated to China (via the personal participation of Smith, and the decision to base R&D and production in Guilin) and local industry partners are very much involved in the innovatory process. Hence, we put forward the following proposition:

> Proposition 1: Domestic institutional and industry linkages (based on *guanxi*) provide a foundation for leveraging the innovative potential of international linkages.

The second insight relates leverage of resources to facilitate development of innovation for international markets. As the firm's developmental trajectory progresses, we find simple strategies and structures built around initial invention and innovation are no longer sufficient, despite the supportive frameworks provided by industry associations, government, and the founders themselves. As with most growth-oriented firms, particularly those that grow from small innovative and entrepreneurial firms dependent on their founders, to those encompassing multiple value chain activities internationally, founder/innovation/product/-oriented structures must transform to accommodate the added complexity that comes from managing more diverse and dissipated resources (Kellermans et al. 2016). With this in mind, collaborative activity, while encouraging earlier innovation, could no longer ensure competitiveness as greater control and resources were needed during the commercialization and internationalization expansion stages of the innovative process.

In the case of Monk Fruit Corp., the next stage was achieved through acquisition of key partners (local and foreign) rather than solely collaboration, as well as the effective management of a more complex web of linkages with foreign firms internationally. Therefore, we propose that innovation can be leveraged more effectively through both collaboration *and* control at the organizational level. This involves a dynamic and evolutionary process that seeks to internalize core advantages relating to innovation, but is quite different approach to that taken by the Western MNE (Dunning 2006; Rugman and Li 2007; Li 2007).

With regard to the acquisition of BioVittoria by Chinese investors, one could argue that this simply addressed failure to attract capital through a New Zealand IPO. Such a conclusion would not be untoward; but using abductive reasoning, we believe that there are more dynamic influences at play that reflect the ultimate predominance of political over social influences. We suggest that the politico-economic policy of the Chinese government towards growing international firms would have been extremely supportive of Chinese investors taking over an innovative joint venture, particularly one that had brought benefits to a poor, rural community and promoted Chinese innovation to the world. Essentially, they were buying the intellectual property and the physical assets of the joint venture along with its international connections while shifting control back to Chinese interests. Therefore, we propose:

> Proposition 2: Leverage of innovative capability associated with international linkages is achieved via collaboration based on social ties combined with increasing control (through equity interest in the organization) over time.

The third insight relates to learning as an outcome of the interplay between individual and organizational linkages. Such organizational "wisdom" (Scott-Kennel and von Batenburg 2012) accumulates on the basis of interaction effects of linkages. This reinforces the idea that leverage occurs as a result of interaction between resources and capabilities associated with individual and organizational linkage participants, as demonstrated in this case, rather than exchange and mutual adaptation of the resources themselves, as suggested by resource-based view of the firm and literature on linkages and MNE networks/embeddedness (Barney 1991; Bjorkman and Kock 1995). A focus of this literature is on analysis of linkages at either firm or individual level rather than on interdependence between the two has obscured this relationship. Thus, we propose that incorporating multiple levels of analysis into the empirical study of LLL, with social and political dimensions providing the context to individual and organizational resources, provides a richer and more finely grained view of these interactions as they lead to learning by the emerging multinational. Our third proposition, therefore, is stated as follows:

> Proposition 3: Learning trajectories of emerging multinationals demonstrate path dependency based on interaction effects between individual and organizational linkages, over time.

Incorporating organizational change as innovation through abductive reasoning and analysis reveals important insights for managing the growth associated with innovation, which we believe constitute a valuable contribution to our understanding of the emerging MNE. This contribution can be linked back to two concepts introduced, but not elaborated on, by Mathews (2006a), namely, strategic and organizational innovation.

Strategic innovation can be defined as an organization's process of reinventing or redesigning its corporate strategy to drive business growth, generate value for the company and its customers, and to create competitive advantage. Monk Fruit Corp. (and its predecessor firms) changes its strategy around formality of linkages to facilitate innovation in order to become more competitive internationally. Leveraging partner resources through linkages, and the subsequent innovation that results from these linkages, not only enables the firm to compete internationally, but also influences its innovation and internationalization strategies. This is achieved at Monk Fruit Corp., by leveraging the resources of its Chinese and foreign founders, local suppliers, and foreign professionals.

Our case also illustrates elements of organizational innovation, which is often associated with new organizational methods relating to workplace organization or external relations. Certainly, our evidence demonstrates that change in product/process innovation led to change to the nature of external linkages with partners, and the joint ventures and M&A that have served to internalize these partners as these relationships have developed. We also see evidence of organizational innovation in terms of capital replacement or extension, provided initially through a foreign partner actively involved in innovation through Sino-foreign collaboration (as we might expect with a Chinese Joint Venture), but eventually funded (owned) by Chinese interests who have no real contribution to make in terms of related innovation. Thus, it may be more accurate to describe this as structural innovation in response to the changing resource needs of the firm as it proceeds on its innovation and internationalization trajectory.

Based on our discussion, therefore, we would argue that strategic and organizational innovation are interdependent and essential for emerging multinationals to adapt to the speed of technology change. Further, the ability for latecomer firms to accomplish this through a flexible and dynamic interplay between linkages and leverage of those linkages may constitute a source of competitive advantage. Nimbleness and the ability to innovate products, processes, strategy, and organization are what set apart latecomer firms like Monk Fruit Corp. Thus, we agree with Mathews' view that "latecomers were able to win a place in the emergent global economy, not on the basis of their existing strengths, but on the basis of their capacity to leverage resources from the strengths of others, through making international connections" (2006a, 14). Further, we extend his argument to incorporate dynamic strategic and structural (organizational) innovation by the firm. This is not merely about competing globally through shared resources and collaborative innovation, as suggested by the extant literature, but suggests LLL is inextricably linked to higher order innovative development of strategy and structure within the evolving organization. Thus, we put forward our fourth proposition:

> Proposition 4: LLL not only underpins innovative change at the product/process level of the latecomer firm, but also influences innovation at the strategic and structural levels.

It is also instructive to note that strategic and structural innovations shift the balance of power: initially associated with access to and leverage of innovation provided by the foreign partner and developed in the host country, then as learning occurs, with the competences and competitive positioning of the firm. This is not the same as an emerging MNE acquiring ownership-specific assets in a foreign country for advantage offshore—the most common route for the emerging MNE—but it is a variant of it that has been little explored until now. As learning occurs, we see the power shift from foreign partners to Chinese firm, and in this case this shift is reinforced by eventual and complete Chinese ownership.

In Mathews' (2006a, 2006b) comparison of the OLI and LLL, he highlights the former's bias toward internalization of operations internationally, and the latter's bias toward operations through external linkages. However, it would appear that the latter converges with the former with regard to a shift from linkages based on social capital to formal ownership driven by investment capital. From an institutional perspective, we also see a shift from reliance on social capital to reliance on organizational capital, then investment capital, which is a nuanced view of home country effects (Voss, Buckley and Cross 2010). Specifically, the socially-constructed relationship between the two founders is reinforced by the more formal establishment of Guilin GFS Bio-Tech, then acquisition of BioVittoria and subsequent integration of all three companies, including Guilin Bio-DaDi into Monk Fruit Corp., which serves to capture, control, and cement innovative processes within the organizational structure, rather than through collaboration. Social capital remains important—but not as important—and the venture and the innovations contained within become increasingly Chinese (through ownership) and international (through market expansion) simultaneously. Investment of Chinese capital, a response to resource deficiencies and the growing international success of the firm, reinforces Chinese dominance—not only in the form of ownership, but also with regard to cultural, political, and technological influence—over the venture. Thus, we propose, albeit rather tentatively, our final proposition:

> Proposition 5: Relational power is derived not only from social capital but also institutional influence, with the former tending to the latter over time.

CONCLUSIONS

By extending the LLL framework to include social capital and political influence, we find that the "world's leading monk fruit company – a title which it has earned from more than a decade dedicated to innovation, focus and leadership in the monk fruit industry" (Monk Fruit Corp 2015a)—has been built on the basis of strong local industry connections and the skills of its founders, and has grown through leveraging its own resources and those of international partners. While China's institutional development and industrial complexity have provided impetus for firm growth, it is the company's collaborative approach to business that has most influenced its innovative development.

Further, the establishment and global expansion of this innovative Chinese firm is not only derived from collaborative international network activity, but also firmly rooted in a strong domestic support structure. However, we find that the firm grows out of these collaborative relationships as it develops, internalizing key relationships through acquisition, suggested by Rui and Yip (2008) as "strategic intent." Ultimately, all original partner organizations are integrated into the group structure, as finance and growth become the priority in highly competitive markets. This observation fits well with our understanding of the growth of the firm, from a focus on product/process innovation to international market strategies and then to a structural shift to accommodate growth (Penrose 1959).

The article makes several theoretical contributions to our understanding of how Chinese firms might facilitate innovation through LLL. The case illustrates the unique approach by which enterprises from emerging economies establish international networks and improve their innovation capacity, a dynamic process that captures the advantages of both local innovation and foreign skills, experience and market reach. In line with the latest LLL research on dragon multinationals (Mathews 2017), it highlights the importance of both foreign partners and local linkages to domestically-based innovative activity.

Thus, our results reaffirm the importance of international linkages and leverage for learning through Sino-foreign collaboration, but do not overstate the case. Instead, we find the process of development is inextricably entwined with the process of learning, achieved over time by leveraging linkages with both domestic and foreign partners. We would also concur with Lu et al. (2017) that inward linkages (such as that of Dr. Smith working in China) may be just as important as outward linkages. Specifically, we find that independent R&D coupled with skill in relationship building as applied by the Chinese firm, and the individuals within it through their *guanxi*, underpin innovative capability development and provide the cement for increasingly formal business relationships (Gao, Knight and Ballantyne 2012). We also demonstrate the empirical value of including three levels of linkage associated with innovation in the firm, namely, individual, organizational, and institutional. Over the course of the firm's development, linkages at individual and organizational levels have supported, facilitated, and driven innovation and reinforced institutional linkages, particularly the fundamental role of social capital in the Chinese context (Rao, Pearce and Xin 2005).

Our contributions to this field of enquiry can be illustrated by way of a model (Figure 2), which demonstrates the LLL associated with individual, organizational, and institutional relationships, the process of leverage of these relationships leading to product/process innovation, and the learning over time that contributes to the strategic and structural innovation dynamic as the firm evolves.

This research suffers, of course, from the limitations inherent in exploratory, case-based research, as well as the difficulties in collecting primary data in the Chinese business context. We would have liked to have obtained greater insights into the mechanics of each of the linkages, and the wider motivations behind the eventual sale of BioVittoria and ownership by Chinese equity investors that lay outside of scope of innovation-based linkages formed by the company. We remain intrigued as to what precisely triggers shifts in strategic and organizational innovation (and power) in the latecomer firm, and how this might feed into our current understanding of their unique approaches to acquiring innovative advantage and international market share.

What seems clear is that innovative firms from emerging economies are gaining competitiveness through linkage and leverage possibilities, and their strategies and organizational architectures represent a unique response by rapid adapters to the new conditions of the global networked economy, similar to the "strategic networks" discussed by Gulati et al. (2000). This article has contributed to this very topical area of research by recognizing that the LLL

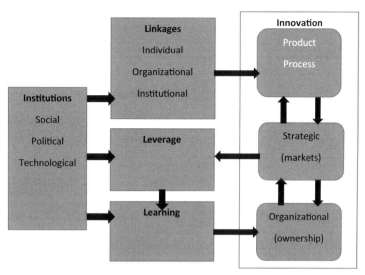

FIGURE 2. Model of Institutions, LLL and Innovation

is a cumulative development process driving internationalization and innovation at multiple levels of dynamic latecomer firm.

WEBSITES

www.biovittoria.com. BioVittoria (no longer available). Accessed 20 June 2013.
www.chinaag.org. ChinaAg www.chinaag.org/agribusiness. Accessed 1 October 2017.
www.glglifetech.com. GLG Life Tech Corp. Accessed 20 September 2017.
www.google.com/patents/WO2008030121A1?cl=en. Patents Office. Accessed 25 September, 2017.
www.layncorp.com. Guilin Layn Natural Ingredients Corp. Accessed 5 October 2017.

REFERENCES

Accenture. 2008. "Multi-Polar World 2: The Rise of the Emerging-market Multinational." Retrieved from http://www.criticaleye.com/insights-detail.cfm?id=351

Aggarwal, R., and T. Agmon. 1990. "The International Success of Developing Ccountry Firms: Role of Government-Directed Comparative Advantage." *Management International Review* 30 (2):163–80.

Ahuja, G. 2000. "The Duality of Collaboration: Inducements and Opportunities in the Formation of Interfirm Linkages." *Strategic Management Journal* 21 (3):317–43. doi:10.1002/(SICI)1097-0266(200003)21:3<317::AID-SMJ90>3.0.CO;2-B.

Anonymous. 2011. "Tate & Lyle Launches PUREFRUIT(TM) Monk Fruit Extract." Baking Management: The Production Magazine for Volume Bakers; Des Plaines, Apr 28.

Barney, J. 1991. "Firm Resources and Sustained Competitive Advantage." *Journal of Management* 17 (1):99–120. doi:10.1177/014920639101700108.

Bjorkman, I., and S. Kock. 1995. "Social Relationships and Business Networks: The Case of Western Companies in China." *International Business Review* 4 (4):519–35. doi:10.1016/0969-5931(95)00023-2.

Boisot, M., and M. W. Meyer. 2008. "Which Way through the Open Door? Reflections on the Internationalization of Chinese Firms." *Management and Organization Review* 4 (3):349–65. doi:10.1111/j.1740-8784.2008.00116.x.

Bridgeman, D. 2015. "How Two Promising Kiwi Biotech Companies Were Lost off-Shore." *National Business Review*. Retrieved from www.nbr.co.nz

Cantwell, J. 2017. "Innovation and International Business." *Industry and Innovation* 24 (1):41–60. doi:10.1080/13662716.2016.1257422.

Chadee, D., R. R. Sharma, and B. Roxas. 2017. "Linking and Leveraging Resources for Innovation and Growth through Collaborative Value Creation: A Study of Indian OSPs." *Asia Pacific Journal of Management* 34 (4): 777–97. doi:10.1007/s10490-016-9485-9.

Chen, K. 2008. "Introducing Foreign Experts to Facilitate a Multi-Billion Dollar Business, Tens of Thousands of Farmers Benefit from European & American Markets." *Guangxi Daily* 2 December (translated from Chinese). Retrieved from https://szbk.gxnews.com.cn/

Cuervo-Cazurra, A., and M. Genc. 2008. "Transforming Disadvantages into Advantages: Developing-Country MNEs in the Least Developed Countries." *Journal of International Business Studies* 39 (6):957–79. doi:10.1057/palgrave.jibs.8400390.

Dubois, A., and J.-E. Gadde. 2002. "Systematic Combining: An Abductive Approach to Case Research." *Journal of Business Research* 55 (7):553–60. doi:10.1016/S0148-2963(00)00195-8.

Dunning, J. H. 2000. "The Eclectic Paradigm as an Envelope for Economic and Business Theories of MNE Activity." *International Business Review* 9 (2):163–90. doi:10.1016/S0969-5931(99)00035-9.

Dunning, J. H. 2003. "Relational Assets, Networks and International Business Activity." In *Alliance and Corporate Management*, edited by J. H. Dunning and G. Boyde, 1–23. Cheltenham, UK: Edward Elgar.

Dunning, J. H. 2006. "Comment on Dragon Multinationals: New Players in 21st Century Globalization." *Asia Pacific Journal of Management* 23 (2):139–41. doi:10.1007/s10490-006-7161-1.

Eisenhardt, K. M., and M. E. Graebner. 2007. "Theory Building from Cases: Opportunities and Challenges." *Academy of Management Journal* 50 (1):25–32. doi:10.5465/amj.2007.24160888.

Fan, P. 2014. "Innovation in China." *Journal of Economic Surveys* 28 (4):725–45. doi:10.1111/joes.12083.

Feng, T. 2015. "Monk Fruit Corp. to Be the Largest Monk Fruit Sweetener Supplier." Dlcy, Retrieved from www.dlcy.com/news/show-509131.html.

Fukuyama, F. 1999. "Social Capital and Civil Society." IMF Conference on Second Generation Reforms. Retrieved from www.imf.org/external/pubs/ft/seminar/1999/reforms/fukuyama.htm#I

Gammeltoft, P., H. Barnard, and A. Madhok. 2010. "Emerging Multinationals, Emerging Theory: Macro- and Micro-Level Perspectives." *Journal of International Management* 16 (2):95–101. doi:10.1016/j.intman.2010.03.001.

Gao, H. Z., D. Knight, and D. Ballantyne. 2012. "Guanxi as a Gateway in Chinese-Western Business Relationships." *Journal of Business & Industrial Marketing* 27 (6):456–67. doi.org/10.1108/08858621211251460 doi:10.1108/08858621211251460.

Gioia, D., K. Corley, and A. Hamilton. 2013. "Seeking Qualitative Rigor in Inductive Research: Notes on the Gioia Methodology." *Organizational Research Methods* 16 (1):15–31. doi:10.1177/1094428112452151.

Giroud, A., and J. Scott-Kennel. 2009. "MNE Linkages in International Business: A Framework for Analysis." *International Business Review* 18 (6):555–65. doi:10.1016/j.ibusrev.2009.07.004.

Guilin Evening News. 2016. "He Introduces an Oriental Fruit from Guilin to the World." Retrieved from http://www.yiwu51.com/wbtd/1969.html.

Gulati, R., N. Nohria, and A. Zaheer. 2000. "Strategic Networks." *Strategic Management Journal* 21 (3):203–15. doi:10.1002/(SICI)1097-0266(200003)21:3<203::AID-SMJ102>3.0.CO;2-K.

Hagedoorn, J., and J. Schakenraad. 1994. "The Effect of Strategic Technology Alliances on Company Performance." *Strategic Management Journal* 15 (4):291–309. doi:10.1002/smj.4250150404.

Huang, C.-H., and Y.-C. Tsang. 2016. "Extending the LLL through an Institutional Based View: Acer as a Dragon MNE." *Asia Pacific Journal of Management* 34 (4):799–821.

Huff, L., and L. Kelley. 2003. "Levels of Organizational Trust in Individualist versus Collectivist Societies: A Seven-Nation Study." *Organization Science* 14 (1):81–90. doi:10.1287/orsc.14.1.81.12807.

Jick, T. 1979. "Mixing Qualitative and Quantitative Methods: Triangulation in Action." *Administrative Science Quarterly* 24 (4):602–11. doi:10.2307/2392366.

Jindra, B., A. Giroud, and J. Scott-Kennel. 2009. "Subsidiary Roles, Vertical Linkages and Economic Development: Lessons from Transition Economies." *Journal of World Business* 44 (2):167–79. doi:10.1016/j.jwb.2008.05.006.

Kellermans, F., J. Walter, T. R. Crook, B. Kemmerer, and V. Narayanan. 2016. "The Resource-Based View in Entrepreneurship: A Content-Analytical Comparison of Researchers' and Entrepreneurs' Views." *Journal of Small Business Studies* 54 (1):26–48. doi:10.1111/jsbm.12126.

Li, P. P. 2007. "Toward an Integrated Theory of Multinational Evolution: The Evidence of Chinese Multinational Enterprises as Latecomers." *Journal of International Management* 13 (3). doi:10.1016/j.intman.2007.05.004.

Li, M., D. Li, M. Lyles, and S. Liu. 2016. "Chinese MNEs' Outward FDI and Home Country Productivity: The Moderating Effect of Technology Gap." *Global Strategy Journal* 6 (4):289–308. doi:10.1002/gsj.1139.

Liu, X., and T. Buck. 2009. "The Internationalization Strategies of Chinese Firms: Lenovo and Boe." *Journal of Chinese Economics and Business Studies* 7 (2):167–81. doi:10.1080/14765280902847627.

Lu, J., X. Ma, L. Taksa, and Y. Wang. 2017. "From LLL to IOL: Moving Dragon Multinationals Research Forward." *Asia Pacific Journal of Management* 34 (4):757–68. doi:10.1007/s10490-017-9542-z.

Luo, Y., and S. L. Wang. 2012. "Foreign Direct Investment Strategies by Developing Country Multinationals: A Diagnostic Model for Home Country Effects." *Global Strategy Journal* 2 (3):244–61. doi:10.1111/j.2042-5805.2012.01036.x.

Mathews, J. A. 2002a. "Competitive Advantages of the Latecomer Firm: A Resource-Based account of Industrial Catch-up Strategies." *Asia Pacific Journal of Management* 19 (4):467–88. doi:10.1023/A:1020586223665.

Mathews, J. A. 2002b. *Dragon Multinational: A New Model for Global Growth.* Cary, NC: Oxford University Press. doi:10.1007/s10490-006-6113-0.

Mathews, J. A. 2006a. "Dragon Multinationals: New Players in 21st Century Globalization." *Asia Pacific Journal of Management* 23 (1):5–27. doi:10.1007/s10490-006-6113-0.

Mathews, J. A. 2006b. "Response to Professors Dunning and Narula." *Asia Pacific Journal of Management* 23 (2):153–5. doi:10.1007/s10490-006-7163-z.

Mathews, J. A. 2017. "Dragon Multinationals Powered by Linkage, Leverage and Learning: A Review and Development." *Asia Pacific Journal of Management* 34 (4):769–75. doi:10.1007/s10490-017-9543-y.

Meyer, K. 2007. "Asian Contexts and the Search for General Theory in Management Research: A Rejoinder." *Asia Pacific Journal of Management* 24 (4):527–34. doi:10.1007/s10490-007-9053-4.

Miles, M., and A. Huberman. 1994. *Qualtitative Data Analysis.* 2nd ed. Thousand Oaks: CA: Sage Publishers, Inc.

Mingjiang, L. 2008. "China Debates Soft Power." *The Chinese Journal of International Politics* 2 (2):287–308. doi:10.1093/cjip/pon011.

Monk Fruit Corp. 2015a. Company History. Retrieved from onkfruitcorp.com/our-history. Accessed 27 November 2017.

Monk Fruit Corp. 2015b. (b) Supply-chain. http://monkfruitcorp.com/supply-chain. Accessed 27 November 2017.

Monk Fruit Corp. 2015c. (c) Company Milestones. http://monkfruitcorp.com/leadership-innovation. Accessed 27 November 2017.

Monk Fruit Corp. 2017. Product. www.monkfruitcorp.cn. Accessed 27 November 2017 (translated from Chinese).

Narula, R. 2006. "Globalization, New Ecologies, New Zoologies, and the Purported Death of the Eclectic Paradigm." *Asia Pacific Journal of Management* 23 (2):143–51. doi:10.1007/s10490-006-7162-0.

National Bank Country Calendar. 2010. Available at www.throng.co.nz/tag/the-national-bank-country-calendar/, accessed 10 September 2017.

Osborne, E., and M. Benson-Rea. 2014. "Sweet Success? The Internationalization of BioVittoria." In *Cases in International Business Strategy: A New Zealand Perspective.* eds. J. Scott-Kennel and M. Akoorie, 1–7. Hamilton, New Zealand: MI Publishing.

Peng, M. W. 2001. "The Resource-Based View and International Business." *Journal of Management* 27 (6):803–29. doi:10.1016/S0149-2063(01)00124-6.

Penrose, E. 1959. *Theory of the Growth of the Firm.* Oxford, UK: Basil Blackwell.

PRNewswire, 2017. "All Natural Food and Drink Market, 2017-2027." Retrieved from www.prnewswire.com/news-releases/all-natural-food–drink-market-report-2017-2027-300498648.html

Professional Services. 2012. "McNeil Nutritionals Leverages BioVittoria's Monk Fruit Extract in New Natural Sweetener." Professional Services Close-Up; Jacksonville, August 31.

Rao, A., J. Pearce, and K. Xin. 2005. "Governments, Reciprocal Exchange and Trust among Business Associates." *Journal of International Business Studies* 36 (1):104–18. doi:10.1057/palgrave.jibs.8400116.

Rugman, A. M., and J. Li. 2007. "Will China's Multinationals Succeed Globally or Regionally?" *European Management Journal* 25 (5):333–43. doi: doi:10.1016/j.emj.2007.07.005.

Rui, H., and G. S. Yip. 2008. "Foreign Acquisitions by Chinese Firms: A Strategic Intent Perspective." *Journal of World Business* 43 (2):213–26. doi:10.1016/j.jwb.2007.11.006.

Scott-Kennel, J., and Z. von Batenburg. 2012. "The Role of Knowledge and Learning in the Internationalization of Professional Service Firms." *The Service Industries Journal* 32 (10):1–24. doi:10.1080/.02642069.2012.665897

Siggelkow, N. 2007. *"Persuasion with Case Studies." Academy of Management Journal* 50 (1):20–4.

Sinkovics, R. R., E. Penz, and P. N. Ghauri. 2008. "Enhancing the Trustworthiness of Qualitative Research in International Business." *Management International Review* 48 (6):689–713. doi:10.1007/s11575-008-0103-z.

Stuart, T. E. 2000. "Inter-Organizational Alliances and the Performance of Firms: A Study of Growth and Innovation Rates in a High-Technology Industry." *Strategic Management Journal* 21 (8):791–811. doi:10.1002/1097-0266(200008)21:8<791::AID-SMJ121>3.0.CO;2-K.

Sun, Y., and Y. Zhou. 2011. "Innovation and Inter-Firm Technological Networking: Evidence from China's Information Communication Technology Industry." *Erdkunde* 65 (1):55–70. doi:10.3112/erdkunde.2011.01.05.

Thite, M., A. Wilkinson, P. Budhwar, and J. A. Mathews. 2016. "Internationalization of Emerging Indian Multinationals: Linkage, Leverage and Learning (LLL) Perspective." *International Business Review* 25 (1):435–43. doi:10.1016/j.ibusrev.2015.06.006.

Tiwari, S. K., S. Sen, and R. Shaik. 2016. "Internationalization: A Study of Small Firms from Emerging Markets." *Journal of Developing Areas* 50 (6):355–64. doi:10.1353/jda.2016.0135.

Voss, H., P. J. Buckley, and A. R. Cross. 2010. "The Impact of Home Country Institutional Effects on the Internationalization Strategy of Chinese Firms." The *Multinational Business Review* 18 (3):25–48. doi:10.1108/1525383X201000014.

Wang, M. Y. 2002. "The Motivations behind China's Government-Initiated Industrial Investments Overseas." *Pacific Affairs* 75 (2):187–206. doi:10.2307/4127182.

Yeganeh, K. H. 2016. "An Examination of the Conditions, Characteristics and Strategies Pertaining to the Rise of Emerging Markets Multinationals." *European Business Review* 28 (5):600–26. doi:10.1108/EBR-10-2015-0129.

Yin, R. K. 2014. "Case Study Research: Design and Methods." In *Sage Publications*, edited by 5th ed. Thousand Oaks, CA: Inc. doi:10.1108/EBR-10-2015-0129.

APPENDIX A

Linkage, Leverage and Learning at Monk Fruit Corp.

Linkage	Leverage (resources)	Learning (innovation, growth)
Garth Smith and Stephen LeFebvre	• Smith (NZ): experience relating to innovation and quality enhancement in NZ kiwifruit industry; expertise in horticultural and botanical product development in food industry. • LeFebvre (US): sales and marketing skills from the US nutraceutical industry.	2003 Establishment of BioVittoria
Fusheng Lan and Garth Smith	• Fusheng Lan (China): monk fruit cultivation expertise. 30+ awards and over 70 published papers in the botanical field; 30+ years' work experience in Guangxi Province, strong and stable relationships with local government and farmers. • Prior to 2001, former Vice-Director of Guangxi Institute of Botany of the Chinese Academy of Sciences CEO of Guilin DaDi (after 2001), Guilin Bio-Tech Co. Ltd (after 2004) supervisor Guilin Lijiang Rural Cooperative Bank, member Guilin Municipal Committee, Vice Chairman Guangxi Association of Overseas and Returned Scholars, Vice Chairman Guilin Plant Extraction Association, and Chairman Guilin Monk Fruit Association. • Study, research, and work experience in the United States, Australia, New Zealand, Belgium, the Netherlands, Luxembourg, Italy, France and Germany. • Garth Smith (NZ): as above, plus horticultural business experience; 18-year involvement in the China's medicinal plant industry.	2004 Establishment of Guilin GFS Bio-Tech Co. Ltd. Access to social networks, commercial opportunities and government networks in China. 2010 Smith developed sweetener extraction method for monk fruit (PureLo: natural calorie free sweetener)
Guilin GFS Bio-Tech and foreign professionals	• Guilin GFS Bio-Tech (China) R&D and production of monk fruit-based ingredients. • Foreign professionals (multiple countries): international experience; expertise	2006 Rapid manufacturing technology for high purity monk fruit glycosides 2007 Invented and commercialized a technique for making monk fruit extract with at least 40% purity (the content of mogroside V) 2008 Extraction technology of monk fruit mogroside Monk fruit controlled atmosphere cold storage technology. 2010 US FDA-GRAS approval. 2012 Invented process for making a clean tasting, stable monk fruit juice Monk fruit concentrate production technology. 2013 Deionized monk fruit concentrate production technology. Monk fruit by-products secondary production technology. Patent for extraction technology of monk fruit mogroside. 2015 Patent for monk fruit extract and extraction method.
Guilin GFS Monk Fruit Corp. and foreign professionals	• Monk Fruit Corp.: R&D and production of monk fruit-based ingredients (Guilin GFS Bio-Tech); seedling manufacturer; seedling culture R&D (Guilin DaDi) • Foreign professional: international experience; expertise	
Guilin DaDi and Guilin GFS Bio-Tech	• Guilin GFS Bio-Tech (China): licensed import/export qualification for monk fruit products; R&D and production of monk fruit-based ingredients. • Guilin DaDi (China): biotechnology D&R; seedling R&D and production.	2007 Invented and commercialized tissue culture technology for monk fruit seedlings. 2009 Developed large scale monk fruit orchards.

(Continued)

APPENDIX A
(*Continued*).

BioVittoria and Tate & Lyle	• Leveraged strategic partnership with Tate & Lyle (one of the world's largest food ingredient companies, 2010 to 2015).	Pioneered the use of environmentally-friendly orchard technology (e.g. drip irrigation for reducing water and fertilizer usage). 2010 Developed monk fruit standardized cultivation technique. 2013 Developed and commercialized technology for spray pollination of monk fruit.
Guilin GFS Bio-Tech, BioVittoria and Guilin DaDi	• Guilin Bio-Tech (China): licensed import/export qualification for monk fruit products; R&D and production of monk fruit-based ingredients. • BioVittoria (Chinese affiliate of the New Zealand company): R&D of monk fruit-based sweeteners; marketing monk fruit-based sweeteners. • Guilin DaDi (China): seedling manufacturer; seedling culture R&D	2010- Marketing and distribution 2012 BioVittoria become ingredient supplier for McNeil Nutritionals 2015 Formed Guilin GFS Monk Fruit Corporation. Tripartite collaborative relationship: Guilin DaDi provides high quality monk fruit seeds; Guilin GFS Bio-Tech organizes monk fruit planting via Guilin Monk Fruit Association, process raw monk fruit and produce monk fruit-based products while provides R&D base for the (former) BioVittoria technique team; and BioVittoria provides extraction technique for sweeteners to Guilin Bio-Tech, and takes responsibility for marketing products produced by Guilin Bio-Tech.
Guilin DaDi and foreign MNEs outside China	• Guilin DaDi (as part of Monk Fruit Corp.): seedling manufacturer; seedling culture R&D • Foreign MNE: international experience; expertise	2015 Monk fruit multi-storied culture technique
Monk Fruit Corp. and foreign MNEs outside China Guilin GFS Bio-Tech and Monk Fruit Association	• Monk Fruit Corp.: product/technique patents • Foreign MNE: expertise in applying for FDA-GRAS approval • Guilin GFS Bio-Tech (China): licensed import/export qualification for monk fruit products; R&D and production of monk fruit-based ingredients. • Monk Fruit Association (China) provided training and support for growers.	2016 The monk fruit extract attained US FDA-GRAS approval as a sweetener including in baby food 2006 Helped the company establish a positive reputation in the community and as such, obtain legitimacy and trust from the Chinese government. Ensured strict quality and quantity control for monk fruit ingredient production
Guilin GFS Bio-Tech and NZ government	• Guilin GFS Bio-Tech (China): China-New Zealand JV: licensed import/ export qualification for monk fruit products; R&D and production of monk fruit-based ingredients. • NZ government: capital and policy support	2008 Guilin GFS Bio-Tech received investment from the New Zealand Government. Completed the first purpose-built monk fruit processing facility near Guilin.

Sources: TVNZ, 2010; Osborne and Benson-Rea 2014; Monk Fruit Corp. 2015a, 2015c; 桂林晚报 (Guilin Evening News), 2016; Lan, personal communications, 2017.

Foreign Ownership and External Knowledge Acquisition: A Comparison between International Subsidiaries and Local Firms in China

Zhi Yang and Tian Wei

Abstract: This study examines the relationship between foreign ownership and External Knowledge Acquisition (EKA) in China, and posits that international subsidiaries and local firms exhibit different rationales with regard to EKA. Using nationwide enterprise survey data on 320 Chinese firms, this study tests a model developed from resource dependency theory and institutional theory. We find that foreign ownership positively affects EKA, and that this relationship is moderated by both institution legislation hazards and contract enforcement hazards but with contrasting effects: the positive moderation of the former but the negative one of the latter. This study also provides important implications for the managers of international subsidiaries and local firms regarding their knowledge acquisition strategies.

Until now, Elon Musk's automaker has invested in huge and modern manufacturing facilities in America. Now, it's looking to spread those operations to China.

—Jamie Condliffe, June 22, 2017, MIT Technology Review

Tesla has reached an agreement with the Chinese government in Shanghai to build a production facility in the city's free-trade zone, potentially giving the carmaker a unique edge in the world's largest market for electric vehicles.

—David Z. Morris October 22, 2017, Fortune

INTRODUCTION

In the past, foreign Multi-national corporations (MNCs) have only been able to avoid tariffs in China by forming joint ventures with local manufacturers, which often include technology-sharing provisions. This policy puts technologically innovative foreign MNCs at very real risk for damaging intellectual property theft, and even more Chinese competition. However, recently, the Chinese government has allowed foreign MNCs to own 100% of their subsidiaries to compete with local firms, such as Tesla's factory in Shanghai. With a rising role of international subsidiaries in the Chinese market, in order to compete efficiently, External Knowledge Acquisition (EKA) is critical for both internal subsidiaries and local firms.

The reliance on external sources of knowledge in firms' research and development (R&D) is acknowledged to be indispensable for the success of innovation (Calantone and Stanko 2007; Laursen, Masciarelli, and Prencipe 2012; Linder, Jarvenpaa, and Davenport 2003). Its significance was articulated by Marshall in 1890, i.e., external knowledge, which is defined as the knowledge outside the boundary of a firm, can be "taken up by others and combined with suggestions of their own; and thus becomes the source of yet more new ideas" (Marshall 1890). External knowledge sourcing supplements focal firms with novel ideas and different solutions that can partially alleviate the challenges that firms face, such as shorter product life cycles, faster product renewal periods, and increasing R&D costs (Rigby and Zook 2002). It also helps these firms to integrate their technology with the local market demands and so increases their legitimacy in the local community (Berchicci 2013; Husted, Montiel, and Christmann 2016). Both international subsidiaries and local firms are actively involved in EKA for innovation. Whether a local firm or an international subsidiary is more active in acquiring external knowledge, however, remains debatable (Ju et al. 2013; Sheth 2011).

Customarily, the foreign ownership of international subsidiaries is often associated with the degree of liability of foreignness in the host country (Denk, Kaufmann, and Roesch 2012; Zaheer 1995; Zhang, Li, and Hitt 2007). To overcome the liability of foreignness, international subsidiaries must acquire local technology and products to adapt to the local needs (Kuemmerle 1997). From resource dependency theory, they should acquire a rich knowledge of the local market and social networks to reduce their reliance on the external context in product and process innovation (Elango 2009; Rangan and Drummond 2004). However, local firms also require knowledge from external sources to facilitate their innovation for a variety of reasons: explore the market (Chesbrough and Crowther 2006), create knowledge (Van de Vrande, Lemmens, and Vanhaverbeke 2006), absorb missing or complementary knowledge, enlarge its social networks, and reduce costs (Hoffman and Schlosser 2001; Mohr and Spekman 1994). Thus, due to their distinct motives, examining and comparing the reliance of international subsidiaries and local firms on EKA in innovation is compelling and imperative.

Interestingly, the relationship between foreign ownership and external knowledge sourcing may vary according to different institutional components due to the complexity and obstacles existing within the institutional environments (Lawrence and Lorsch 1967; Feinberg and Gupta 2009). By revealing the contingent nature from an institutional perspective, we propose that firms face two types of institutional hazards with regard to EKA for innovation: institution legislation hazards and contract enforcement hazards.

First, institution legislation hazards refer to difficulties associated with the act of making or enacting the laws of an institution (Treaties of the European Union 2010). Its effects arise due to two major reasons. The first one is the unpredictability of the policy, the laws of contract, and those related to business operations. The second is the conflicting interests between the local government and international subsidiaries. Second, contract enforcement hazards are obstacles in the circumstances surrounding the formation of the contract to make it enforceable (North and Thomas 1973; North 1981). It affects EKA in terms of creating implicit knowledge through external collaboration and unfavorable local environments. Therefore, both institution legislation and contract enforcement hazards create different contexts and play a moderating role in utilizing external knowledge. Unfortunately, prior studies have often confounded those with institutional hazards (Barro 1991; Deng 2003; Elango 2009; Li and Zhong 2003).

To address these research gaps, we examine the EKA in facilitating the innovation of international subsidiaries and local firms with regard to the effects of institution legislation and contract enforcement hazards in China. As an emerging economy, China is quickly rising up the global ranks in a number of intellectual property-heavy sectors, with an increasing number of foreign-invested R&D centers, from under 200 in the year 2000 to 1,300 in 2010 (*Business Times* 2011[1]). In particular, we address the following major research questions: First, which type of firm relies more on external knowledge in innovation, international subsidiaries or local firms, and how does foreign ownership affect EKA? Second, how do institution legislation and contract enforcement hazards moderate the reliance on external knowledge by international subsidiaries? We used nationwide enterprise survey data on 320 Chinese firms, gathered by the World Bank in China, to test our proposed hypotheses.

This study contributes to the existing literature in three aspects. First, from a resource dependency perspective, our study fills the gap regarding the role of foreign ownership in EKA in emerging countries. Previously, scholars selected ownership, location, and internalization (OLI) and institutional theory to explain the effects of foreign ownership on EKA for innovation in international business (Dunning 1988; Luo 2001; Zaheer 1995). In our study, we argue that external knowledge is critical for the success of both international subsidiaries and local firms. However, compared with local firms, international subsidiaries rely more on external knowledge in innovation in the host countries and therefore tend to acquire more external knowledge.

Second, this study integrates resource dependency theory and institutional theory by unraveling the confounding moderating effects of institutional hazards on EKA for innovation. Interestingly, institution legislation and contract enforcement hazards have contrasting effects: a positive one in the case of the former but a negative one in the case of the latter. Third, the findings also shed light on the field of innovation and knowledge management. External knowledge, as an important source of open innovation, becomes more indispensable for firms with foreign ownership. Therefore, international subsidiaries are more active in collaborating with local partners.

THEORETICAL DEVELOPMENT

Resource Dependency Theory of External Knowledge Acquisition (EKA) for Innovation

Resource dependency theory characterizes the firm as an open system, dependent on contingencies in the external environment (Pfeffer and Salancik 1978). It helps to explain how (albeit constrained by the external environment) organizations strive to reduce their environmental interdependence and uncertainty through enacting their environment (Gaffney, Kedia, and Clampit 2013). Accordingly, a firm must respond to the environment (deal with contingencies) by managing its inter-organizational relations in order to acquire and maintain the resources (tangible and intangible) crucial to the firm's ability to compete or survive in the market (Hillman, Wither, and Collins 2009).

EKA for innovation refers to a sourcing strategy whereby a firm acquires knowledge about innovation from external parties (Calantone and Stanko 2007; Linder, Jarvenpaa, and Davenport 2003). This is one of the key pillars of the open innovation paradigm, in which the R&D structure should be seen as an open system (Chesbrough 2003). Firms can and should absorb external ideas to advance their technology beyond their firm boundaries (Chesbrough, Vanhaverbeke, and West 2006). According to resource dependency theory, firms are more likely to develop external connections in various forms to acquire crucial outside resources to mitigate the risk of dependency and uncertainty stemming from these uncontrolled external resources in innovation. In an emerging economy, local firms and international subsidiaries face different constraints from the external environment (Luo 2001, 2002). Therefore, their dependencies on external resources are not the same. The nature of foreign ownership gives international subsidiaries distinct motives for external technology sourcing—for example, local adaption to alleviate the liability of foreignness (Asmussen 2009; Barnard 2010), the leverage of their new and relevant knowledge (Cantwell 1994), and protection of their position in MNCs (Pearce 1999; Mudambi 2011). These complicated motives drive international subsidiaries to behave differently from local firms in terms of external technological knowledge sourcing.

Institutional Theory of EKA for Innovation

Institutional theory addresses the interplay between institutions and organizations and considers the processes by which structures, including schemes, rules, norms, and routines, become established as authoritative guidelines for social behavior (North 1990; Scott 2004). Whereas resource dependency theory focuses on the influence of external resources on organizational behavior, institutional theory emphasizes the formal and legal aspects of government structure (Kraft 2007). Undoubtedly, firm behavior and strategies are not only determined by their dependency on external resources but also heavily impacted by the institutional constraints from the context in which they exist (Peng, Wang, and Jiang 2008).

Feinberg and Gupta's (2009) argument on institutional hazards explains the contingencies of acquiring external knowledge. The term "institutional hazards," which is used interchangeably with "country risk," originates from the obstacles regarding the substance and implementation of future government policies (Feinberg and Gupta 2009; Henisz 2000; Uhlenbruck et al. 2006). With this logic, firms should alleviate the risks to its knowledge transfer posed by institutional hazards, which operate in two distinct categories: First, institution legislation hazards, which refer to the enactment and establishment of policy, the laws of contract, and those related to business operations, and, second, contract enforcement hazards, which are associated with the enforcement of the terms and conditions in the contract. Based on these definitions, institution legislation hazards are about the difficulties in the establishment of rules and policies. Contract enforcement hazards are about the difficulties in the enforcement of rules and policies, which is the execution of established legislation.

Contract enforcement hazards are distinct from institution legislation hazards

These two types of hazards should have different impacts on EKA. In an emerging economy, such as China, the underdeveloped legal system creates an uncertain environment for new product development due to the lack of intellectual property protection (Hoskisson et al. 2000). The unpredictability of the institutional environment exerts pressure on international subsidiaries due to their foreign ownership feature. International subsidiaries should respond differently toward institution legislation hazards and contract enforcement hazards. As a result, resource dependency and institutional theory are likely jointly to affect EKA in the context of an emerging economy.

HYPOTHESES

Our study integrates resource dependency theory and institutional theory to explain the phenomenon of EKA between international subsidiaries and local firms. First, resource dependency theory is employed to explain our main hypotheses. Firms tend to optimize the reliance on external resources in order to reduce uncertainties. International subsidiaries and local firms face distinct levels of uncertainties in their environment. This dichotomy of foreign ownership indicates international subsidiaries and local firms have contrasting attitudes towards EKA for innovation. We further investigate international subsidiaries to provide a detailed capture of the effects of foreign ownership on EKA. Second, institutional theory expects that institutional legislation and contract enforcement hazards affect the relationship between foreign ownership and EKA for innovation. These two moderating effects have been explored to provide a complete picture EKA for innovation in emerging markets.

EKA for Innovation

We argue that international subsidiaries prefer to engage in more EKA in innovation compared with their local counterparts. First, foreign ownership predicts the foreign firms' commitment to and relative control over their subsidiaries (Shleifer and Vishny 1997; Yan and Gray 1994). This leads to internal consistency between the international subsidiaries and their foreign parent. The more similar the international subsidiaries are to their MNCs, the greater pressure they confront in delivering products to local customers in the host country (Gupta and Govindarajan 2000). External knowledge is, therefore, more effective in facilitating innovation for developing products in their competition with local firms. In order to reduce their liability of foreignness, international subsidiaries should utilize external knowledge for innovation from the environment. Only through greater EKA can international subsidiaries reduce their reliance on the external environment in the host country.

Second, in an emerging economy, compared with local firms, international subsidiaries have the advantage of being able to absorb internal knowledge from their MNCs, such as advanced proprietary technology, immobile strategic assets (e.g., brands, local distribution networks) and other capabilities (Back, Parboteeah, and Nam 2014; Deng 2003; Li and Zhong 2003; Warner, Hong, and Xu 2004; Zhang 2003). International subsidiaries, therefore, face more pressure from the local environment due to the persistence and inertia toward their MNCs. In the local market, international subsidiaries should acquire new insights and knowledge from external sources to enable them to adapt their transferred products or capabilities to the local environment (Johnsen et al. 2006; Ren et al. 2014). This leads to a greater reliance by international subsidiaries on external knowledge sourcing. Therefore, local adaption facilitates and evokes more EKA, thereby enabling international subsidiaries to mitigate their dependency on external sourcing.

Third, in emerging economies, local firms can experience a "liability of localness" (Husted, Montiel, and Christmann 2016), which refers to "the added costs in doing business at home" (Jiang and Stening 2013). For example, compared with their counterparts in developed markets, it is relatively difficult for local firms to develop advanced technology with their local partners due to the limitation of the local R&D capabilities (Fan 2006). They also face significant challenges in institutional frameworks due to economic reforms (Meyer, Mudambi, and Narula 2011).

In order to compete efficiently, local firms may not rely greatly on their open innovation system, but tend to compete on managing resources they own, such as cost advantage. However, as their competitors, international subsidiaries do not have the advantage of cost leadership in emerging markets. Therefore, in order to compete with local firms, international subsidiaries have to make more efforts on developing local products and services by integrating their advanced technology and managerial resources transferred from their MNCs with local knowledge. Thus, in an emerging economy, the acquisition of external knowledge is critical for international subsidiaries in the market competition.

These arguments suggest that it is necessary and imperative for international subsidiaries to acquire external technology more than it is for local firms. Their reliance on external knowledge for innovation becomes greater due to their increased liability of foreignness and requirements with regard to local adaption. On the one hand, from the resource dependency perspective, international subsidiaries should acquire external knowledge to reduce this reliance. On the other hand, in an emerging economy, local firms do not rely greatly on their external knowledge in competition due to efficiency. All else being equal, we expect that international subsidiaries tend to engage in more EKA compared with local firms.

Hypothesis 1a: International subsidiaries tend to acquire more external knowledge than local firms do.

Foreign ownership indicates that MNCs have control over their international subsidiaries (Short 1994). Greater foreign ownership reflects that subsidiaries are under stronger control by, and have closer linkages with, their MNCs (Zhang, Li, and Hitt 2007), but experience a larger distance from the local organizational practices. The liability of foreignness is largely increased and more internal knowledge can be transferred to international subsidiaries with greater foreign ownership. Thus, building new expertise and learning local knowledge are more significant to the innovation of international subsidiaries when the degree of foreign ownership is greater. All else being equal, we expect that international subsidiaries with greater foreign ownership will tend to rely more on EKA for innovation, which creates a positive relationship with EKA.

Hypothesis 1b: The greater the foreign ownership of international subsidiaries, the more EKA occur.

The Moderating Roles of Institution Legislation and Contract Enforcement Hazards

In emerging economies, the institutional hazards increase due to the incomplete market regulations, inefficient bureaucracy, and unpredictable government actions (Bartlett and Ghoshal 1989; Jensen and Szulanski 2004; Nohria and Ghoshal 1997). Firms should alleviate the risks associated with institutional hazards in their external technology sourcing. Institution legislation hazards, as important aspects of institutional hazards, are mostly driven by the unpredictability of the policy, the laws of contract, and those related to business operations. We argue that institution legislation hazards positively moderate the relationship between foreign ownership and EKA for innovation.

First, the unpredictability of institution legislation in an emerging economy increases the reliance of international subsidiaries on local external knowledge for innovation. As a newcomer in the host country, international subsidiaries lack specific institutional and host-market knowledge of how to adapt their existing products to local business practices (Denk, Kaufmann, and Roesch 2012; Elango 2009). Even though this can be found on government websites or in public documents, the development nature of an emerging economy means that this knowledge is highly changeable. The success of international subsidiaries relies on external knowledge sourcing. Given the unpredictable nature of external knowledge, international subsidiaries should timely update their external knowledge on the changing market to updating their products in order to stabilize their reliance. Therefore, more external knowledge is required for the growth of international subsidiaries.

Second, institution legislation is regarded as a main function of government (Eskridge, Frickey, and Garrett 2007). Its establishment is not on behalf of the overall benefits of the country. Local governments interfere and intervene with international subsidiaries, and their MNCs potentially limit their opportunities in return (Nolan 2001; Li, Poppo, and Zhou 2008). As such, local policies and regulations are not favorable to international subsidiaries but share their opportunities and economic rents with local firms. The necessity of EKA for innovation is thus strengthened. Only with a comprehensive understanding of local policies and regulations related to innovation can international subsidiaries appropriately develop their products to compete with local firms. Thus, in order to promote their own growth and profitability, international subsidiaries have a desire to learn from external sources to reduce their constraints set by local government.

These arguments suggest that EKA is more important when the institution legislation hazards are higher due to its unpredictability and the conflicting interests between the local governments and the international subsidiaries. All else being equal, we argue that, if international subsidiaries face higher institution legislation hazards in emerging economies, greater foreign ownership can more positively affect EKA for innovation, which creates a positive moderating relationship.

Hypothesis 2: The relationship between foreign ownership and EKA is more positive when the institution legislation hazards in the host country are more severe.

Contract enforcement hazards occur in countries where the government's commitment to a given structure of taxation and/or regulation, or even a set of property rights, is difficult to enforce (Henisz and Williamson 1999). These become more critical in an emerging economy, which entails a fragile business environment, insufficient legal protection, absent institutional rules, and inefficient bureaucracy (Hitt et al. 2004; Hoskisson et al. 2000; North 1990).

Two types of contact enforcement hazard exist: direct and indirect (Henisz and Williamson, 1999). First, direct contract enforcement hazards are strongly associated with the lack of enforceability of contracts by the local government (Greif 1993). They refer to a situation whereby the local government prefers to behave in an opportunistic manner for its own benefit and convenience. These weak government manners and inefficient bureaucracy means that international subsidiaries cannot simply reduce potentially negative forces by codifying or acting directly to combat them (Back, Parboteeah, and Nam 2014; Boisot and Child 1999; Lin et al. 2009). Furthermore, some of these engagements and interactions contradict the values and beliefs of MNCs, such as corruption (Gao 2006). As such, the enormous challenges posed by the implicit nature of knowledge and confronting values result in a greater reliance on internal knowledge transfer from MNCs to develop advanced products rather than EKA for international subsidiaries.

Second, indirect contract enforcement hazards refer to the obstacles posed by local firms through their relatively strong information-seeking capabilities. Through their own managerial ties, local firms not only obtain access to scarce resources and information to reduce uncertainty (Podolny and Page 1998) but can also influence the development of the strategies of the government officials (Peng and Luo 2000). They may opportunistically approach the local governments with requests to enforce certain regulations but not execute others for their own purpose (Podolny and Page 1998). These unfavorable environments, created by hidden rules, make it more difficult for international subsidiaries to obtain knowledge for innovation from external sources. Therefore, they do not rely heavily on external knowledge in market competition.

These arguments suggest that contract enforcement hazards create tremendous challenges for international subsidiaries, direct and indirect. With higher contract enforcement hazards, the acquisition of external knowledge becomes extremely difficult, and the reliance of international subsidiaries is therefore reduced. We argue that international subsidiaries with greater foreign ownership become less active in acquiring external knowledge for innovation. All else being equal, if international subsidiaries face higher contract enforcement hazards in emerging economies, greater foreign ownership can less positively affect EKA, which creates a negative moderating relationship.

Hypothesis 3: The relationship between foreign ownership and EKA is less positive when the contract enforcement hazards in the host country are more severe.

METHODS

Data

The PIC survey

To test our hypotheses, we use the World Bank's Productivity and the Investment Climate (PIC) survey in China. The purpose of this survey is to improve understanding of the conditions within the local investment climate and how they affect firm-level productivity. The PIC survey has been widely used in existing studies (Saliola and Zanfei 2009; Srholec 2011).

In this study, we selected to use the PIC survey in China, which was conducted from December 2011 to February 2013. China is selected due to its rapid changes and high frequency of new product introduction (Wu and Wu 2014; Wu 2013). In order to innovate proactively, both local firms and international subsidiaries rely on EKA to facilitate innovation. Besides, as a highly complex and dynamic transition economy, the underdeveloped institutions and unpredictable government action of China offers great potential for studying institutional hazards (Luo 2003). Accordingly, a sample of Chinese firms provides a useful empirical setting for testing the relationship between foreign ownership and EKA, and the moderating effects of institutional hazards.

The World Bank employed a stratified random sampling method to guarantee sample representativeness. It utilizes a standardized survey instrument with a uniform questionnaire, which was applied to all respondents. The questions can be separated into two parts. The first part provides information across nine sections, which mainly collect data on the investment climate, infrastructure, sales and suppliers, innovation, and technology from a manager's perspective by interviewing business owners or senior managers. The second part provides supplementary quantitative information, such as production costs, cash flows, balance sheet, workforce statistics, etc. Data were collected by conducting interviews with company accountants and human resource managers. Common method variance was reduced through selecting different respondents from the same firm.

The sample

Our primary data are drawn from the PIC survey, which covers 2,700 firms. Consistent with our research that focuses on product and process innovation, we select the manufacturing sector of the survey, which includes 1,693 firms, with 123 international subsidiaries and 1,570 local firms. In our study, we compare local firms with international subsidiaries in terms of EKA. We select local firms using the propensity score matching method to develop a balanced sample from the survey.

This method ensures an equal probability of foreign ownership for each pair of international subsidiary and local firms (Dehejia and Wahba 2002). It prevents selection bias in the aspects of industry regulations and regional differences. First, in the context of China, some industries are regulated to prohibit international subsidiaries (i.e., firms with foreign ownership). These regulations inherently determine the level of foreign ownership for firms in these industries and affect their strategy in EKA. Therefore, without considering this phenomenon, the "0" foreign ownership sample in our regression can be significantly biased towards the local firms in regulated industries. Second, in China, some regions have better endowment or history of hosting foreign companies in the past, it is more likely that firms in those regions are more likely to be acquired by foreign firms and have higher foreign ownership. When we run the regression, the selected foreign firms then are significant different from local firms due to the regional differences. Therefore, simply using the whole sample may cause serious problem and result in biased results. To overcome this problem, we ensured that the sample we use in the regression is free of the potential selection bias regarding the foreign ownership.

The propensity score matching method was conducted in three steps. First, based on the firm characteristics (e.g., firm age, firm size, industry, and location), we estimated the probability of foreign ownership of each firm using a probit regression model. We constructed *International Subsidiary* as a dummy variable, assigning a value 1 if the firm has foreign ownership, and 0 otherwise. The probit model predicted a propensity score for each firm in the sample. Second, from the propensity score of each international subsidiary, we used the Nearest Neighbor (NN) matching algorithm to select its local matching partners, the ones that have an equivalent propensity by the NN score matching algorithm. It is possible that the matched local firms may be used more than once when multiple international subsidiaries have equal propensity scores. In order to develop a balanced sample, we selected two nearest neighbors of local firms as matching partners. In total, 207 local firms were selected as the matching group.

Third, we combined international subsidiaries with their matched local firms, and further dropped 10 firms with missing values for the variables under study. As a result, our sample contains 320 firms in total, including 122 international subsidiaries and 198 local firms. Therefore, whether a firm has foreign ownership becomes random and we are able to

TABLE 1.
Industry Distribution of the Sample

Industry	Freq.	Percent	Cum.
Food	36	11.25	11.25
Textiles	32	10.00	21.25
Garments	30	9.38	30.63
Chemicals	30	9.38	40.00
Plastics and rubber	21	6.56	46.56
Nonmetallic mineral products	35	10.94	57.50
Basic metals	19	5.94	63.44
Fabricated metal products	27	8.44	71.88
Machinery and equipment	21	6.56	78.44
Electronics	23	7.19	85.63
Motor vehicles	29	9.06	94.69
Other manufacturing	17	5.31	100.00
Total	320	100.00	

mitigate the potential selection bias, which stems from solely selecting international subsidiaries (Dehejia and Wahba 2002).

In total, our sample contains 122 international subsidiaries (38.12%) and 198 local firms (61.88%). In this sample, 47 firms (14.69%) are wholly-owned subsidiaries by foreign MNCs, 67 firms (21%) have foreign ownership of 25% or over but less than 100%, and 8 firms (2.5%) have foreign ownership less than 25%. The rationale that we set 25% foreign ownership as a cut is that the foreign partner is required to contribute a minimum of 25% of the joint venture's capital according to the Chinese joint venture law (Luo 2001). The sample with foreign ownership of 25% or over but less than 100% represent joint ventures. Therefore, we have three types of international subsidiaries in our sample: wholly-owned subsidiaries, joint venture, and subsidiaries with low foreign ownership. The sample covers the following twelve manufacturing sectors (Table 1): Food (11.25%), Textiles (10%), Garments (9.38%), Chemicals (9.38%), Plastics and Rubber (6.56%), Nonmetallic mineral products (10.94), Basic metals (5.94%), Fabricated metal products (8.44%), Machinery and equipment (6.56%), Electronics (7.19%), Motor vehicles (9.06%), and Other manufacturing (5.31%).

Of these 320 sampled firms, 122 (38.13%) have no EKA in their product or process innovation; 44 (13.75%) have the whole spectrum of EKA from suppliers, customers, consultants, universities, R&D institutes, etc.; and 154 (48.13%) have some level of EKA. Two-way tabulation further suggests that there are 81 (66% of 122) international subsidiaries with EKA.

Besides, we also gained data based on market competition from the Annual Census of Industrial Enterprises (ACIE), which has been developed by the China National Bureau of Statistics (CNBS) and utilized for the *China Statistic Yearbook* to generate industrial level indicators (Gao et al. 2010; Ju et al. 2013). This census dataset is used for aggregating firm-level data to the industrial level.

Measurement

Dependent variable

EKA refers to the acquisition of knowledge for a firm's product or process innovation from the external market. In our study, we focus on the width rather than the amount of EKA. First, our study focuses particularly on the EKA for innovation. It has been evident that the integration of external knowledge sources with internal knowledge can greatly increase firm innovativeness (Cassiman and Veugelers 2006; Chesbrough and Teece 1996). Second, from our selected theoretical perspective, namely, resource dependency theory, international subsidiaries face more uncertainties compared with local firms. They are eager to acquire all sorts of external knowledge to reduce uncertainties. Therefore, the number of sources is more critical than the amount for our study.

Similar to Cassiman and Veugelers (2006)'s measurement in the Community Innovation Survey (CIS), which was performed by Eurostat for European Union members, World Bank PICS asked managers to select their sources of external knowledge. These sources include other firms, suppliers, clients, consultants, universities, and research institutions. Their definitions are the same as those illustrated in the literature (Kang and Kang 2014; Love and Mansury 2007; Rothaermel 2001). We coded each item as 0 and 1, indicating whether it has been used as an external source for each sample. We added together the codes for all six items as the measure for EKA, which ranges from 0 to 6 and predicts how widely a firm's knowledge acquisition in its innovation spans external sources.

Independent variable

Foreign Ownership served as the independent variable. It was measured by the percentage of foreign equity share of the company, ranging from 0 to 100%.

Moderating variables

Institutional Hazards are studied from two distinct constructs: *institution legislation hazards* and *contract enforcement hazards*. The managers in this survey were asked "To what degree is the following issue an obstacle to the current operations of your establishment?" (from $0 = $ no obstacle, to $4 = $ a very severe obstacle). The issues include: tax rate, tax administration, business license, political instability, corruption, and courts. Each issue can be understood as an item.

Institution Legislation Hazards were measured by the first three items: tax rate, tax administration, and business license. These reflect the effects of the unpredictability of the local policies, regulations and processes on firms. *Contract Enforcement Hazards* were measured by the other three items: political instability, corruption, and courts. They refer to the obstacles posed by the implicit knowledge of the enforcement of local legal protection and institutional rules (Hitt et al. 2004; Hoskisson et al. 2000; North 1990).

TABLE 2.
Measurement for the Major Constructs

Constructs	Variable	
External Knowledge Acquisition (EKA) We add all the items (each item is a 0/1 dummy) to measure the extent of EKA	1. New product innovation developed in cooperation with suppliers 2. New product innovation developed in cooperation with client firms 3. New product innovation implemented idea from an external source, e.g., consultants, universities, and research institutions 4. New process innovation developed in cooperation with suppliers 5. New process innovation developed in cooperation with client firms 6. New process innovation implemented idea from an external source, e.g. Consultants, universities, and research institutions	

	Items	*Factor Loading*
To what degree the following issue is an obstacle to the current operations of this establishment? (0 = no obstacle, 4 = very severe obstacle)		
Legislation Hazards (Cronbach a = 0.85)	1. Tax rate	0.92
	2. Tax administration	0.94
	3. Business License	0.78
Contract Enforcement Hazards (Cronbach a = 0.77)	1. Political instability	0.72
	2. Corruption	0.88
	3. Courts	0.88

Factor analysis confirms this categorization. The six items can be decomposed into two factors, with 3.19 and 1.29 as their eigenvalue, respectively. Further confirmatory factor analysis suggested sufficient reliability for both measures. The lowest factor loading for institution legislation hazards is 0.77 (business license), and its Cronbach α of institution legislation hazards is 0.85, which indicates satisfactory reliability. Similarly, the lowest factor loading for contract enforcement hazards is 0.72 (political instability), and its Cronbach α of contract enforcement hazards is 0.77, which is above the 0.7 benchmark. A discriminant validity test was also conducted. The shared variance between institution legislation and contract enforcement hazards is 0.19, while the average inter-item correlations within the constructs are 0.66 and 0.53 for the two constructs, respectively, which is considerably above the shared variance. Table 2 shows the measuring questions and reliability of the constructs.

Control variables

A number of firm and market-specific variables were included as controls. *Firm size* was measured by the logarithm of employees. *Firm age* was measured by the logarithm of years since establishment. *Market competition* was measured by the negative value of the normalized Herfindahl index for each industry with census data on all manufacturing firms taken from the China National Statistical Bureau. The Herfindahl index was calculated as the sum of the square terms of each company's market share within a certain industry. The larger the Herfindahl index, the less competition presents in the industry. *Export* was measured by the percentage of exports in the firm's total sales. We also controlled for the differences between

TABLE 3.
Summary Statistics of Variables

Variables	Mean	Std. Dev.	Min	Max	(1)	(2)	(3)	(4)	(5)	(6)	(7)	(8)
(1) External Knowledge Acquisition (EKA)	2.03	2.11	0	6	1.00							
(2) Foreign Ownership	24.72	36.95	0	100	0.12*	1.00						
(3) Legislation Hazards (LH)	0.00	1.00	−0.95	3.37	0.11*	0.08	1.00					
(4) Contract Enforcement Hazards (CEH)	0.00	1.00	−2.10	6.18	0.22***	0.05	0.44***	1.00				
(5) Market Competition (COMP)	0.00	1.00	−2.13	1.01	−0.10	−0.04	−0.01	−0.09	1.00			
(6) Firm age	2.35	0.46	0.00	3.30	0.06	−0.06	0.06	0.02	0.06	1.00		
(7) Firm size	4.74	1.31	1.79	9.62	0.14*	−0.03	0.03	−0.04	0.02	0.14*	1.00	
(8) Export	20.89	30.36	0	100	0.10	0.30***	0.01	0.08	−0.05	−0.09	0.06	1.00

$***p < 0.001$; $**p < 0.01$; $*p < 0.05$.

industries by using two industry dummy variables: *labor-intensive industry* and *knowledge intensive industry*. Table 3 presents the summary statistics of all constructs and variables.

Analytical Approach

EKA, as a dependent variable, is a count number and conforms to Poisson distribution. We, therefore, use Poisson regression rather than OLS regression to test the hypotheses. Table 4 presents the results. Model 1 includes only control variables. Model 2 adds the main effect of foreign ownership. Model 3 adds foreign ownership and its interaction term with institution legislation hazards. Model 4 adds foreign ownership and its interaction term with contract enforcement hazards, and Model 5 adds the main effect and both inter-action terms.

All variables were mean-centered before entering the interaction terms to reduce the potential problem of multi-collinearity (Aiken and West 1991). The interaction term of foreign ownership and institution legislation hazards may be affected by the interaction between contract enforcement hazards and foreign ownership if the latter is not controlled. Therefore, we used a further residual centering procedure, as suggested by Zhang, Li, and Hitt (2007) and Lance (1988), to delineate the confounding effect in Model 3 and Model 4.

This procedure consists of two steps. First, the interaction terms of foreign ownership and institution legislation hazards were regressed on the constructs: foreign ownership, institution legislation hazards, contract enforcement hazards, and the interaction terms of foreign ownership and contract enforcement hazards. Second, the residuals were saved and used instead of the original interaction term in Model 3. A similar procedure was followed in Model 4. First, the interaction term of foreign ownership with contract enforcement hazards was regressed with institution legislation hazards and other components. Second, the original interaction term was replaced by the residual of the regression. However, in Model 5, both interaction terms were considered in the model and controlled for each other's effect simultaneously.

TABLE 4.
Poisson Regression Results of External Knowledge Acquisition (EKA)

	(1)	(2)	(3)	(4)	(5)
Foreign ownership (FO)		0.00**	0.00**	0.00**	0.00***
		(0.00)	(0.00)	(0.00)	(0.00)
FO × LH			0.08*		0.24*
			(0.04)		(0.11)
FO × CEH				−0.08*	−0.24*
				(0.04)	(0.11)
Legislation hazards (LH)	0.011	0.001	−0.01	−0.00	−0.07
	(0.04)	(0.04)	(0.04)	(0.04)	(0.06)
Contract Enforcement hazards (CEH)	0.18***	0.18***	0.19***	0.19***	0.26***
	(0.04)	(0.04)	(0.04)	(0.04)	(0.05)
Market competition	−0.06	−0.06	−0.07	−0.05	−0.06
	(0.05)	(0.05)	(0.05)	(0.05)	(0.05)
Firm age	0.13	0.14	0.12	0.13	0.12
	(0.09)	(0.09)	(0.09)	(0.09)	(0.09)
Firm size	0.11***	0.12***	0.12***	0.12***	0.12***
	(0.03)	(0.03)	(0.03)	(0.03)	(0.03)
Export	0.00	0.00	0.00	0.00	0.00
	(0.00)	(0.00)	(0.00)	(0.00)	(0.00)
Labor intensive Industry	0.10	0.10	0.10	0.11	0.11
	(0.10)	(0.10)	(0.10)	(0.10)	(0.10)
Knowledge Intensive Industry	0.15	0.13	0.13	0.13	0.13
	(0.15)	(0.15)	(0.15)	(0.15)	(0.15)
Constant	−0.29	−0.38	−0.36	−0.36	−0.35
	(0.27)	(0.27)	(0.27)	(0.27)	(0.27)
No. of Obs.	320	320	320	320	320
Pseudo R^2	0.04	0.05	0.05	0.05	0.05
LR Chi^2	55.73	62.18	66.78	67.11	68.92
Prob > Chi^2	0.00	0.00	0.00	0.00	0.00

Standard errors in parentheses.
*$p < 0.05$, **$p < 0.01$, ***$p < 0.001$.

Thus, the residual centering procedure was thus unnecessary and the original interaction terms were kept. We examined the variance inflation factors (VIFs) for all variables, and no VIF exceeds 2, indicating that multi-collinearity is not a problem.

RESULTS

Foreign Ownership and EKA

It was expected that, the greater the share of foreign ownership of the subsidiaries, the greater the possibility that they acquire more external knowledge from the local markets. As Table 4 presents, foreign ownership shows a significantly positive effect on EKA in all models ($b = 0.00$, $p < 0.01$, Model 2; $b = 0.00$, $p < 0.00$, Model 5), which lends support for hypotheses 1a and 1b. These results suggest that foreign ownership has a significantly positive effect on EKA.

Effects of Institution Legislation and Contract Enforcement Hazards

It was predicted that institution legislation hazards positively moderate the relationship between foreign ownership and EKA. The results in Model 3 and Model 5 show that the coefficients for the interaction term of foreign ownership and legislation hazards are positive and significant ($b = 0.08$, $p < 0.05$, Model 3; $b = 0.23$, $p < 0.05$, Model 5). This indicates that the positive effect of foreign ownership on EKA is stronger when more institution legislation hazards exist. Thus, hypothesis 2 is supported.

It was also expected that contract enforcement hazards negatively moderate the main effect between foreign ownership and EKA. The results in Model 4 and Model 5 show that the coefficient for the interaction term of foreign ownership and contract enforcement hazards is negative and statistically significant ($b = -0.08$, $p < 0.05$, Model 2; $b = -0.245$, $p < 0.05$, Model 5). This suggests that the main effect of foreign ownership on EKA is weaker when more contract enforcement hazards are present, and therefore supports hypothesis 3.

Facing the contrasting roles of institution legislation hazards and contract enforcement hazards, the results indicate that institutional hazards should not be considered as an overall effect but that it is worth unlocking its moderating mechanism. This contrasting effect can be explained jointly by resource dependency theory and institutional theory. Institution legislation hazards, which are driven by the unpredictability of policy and the laws of contract and property, increase the necessity for external knowledge to the success of international subsidiaries (Elango 2009). This underpins the importance of international subsidiaries to mitigate the risk of reliance on uncontrollable external resources. Therefore, a positive moderating effect on the main relationship is presented. In contrast, contract enforcement hazards arise from hidden rules, unique characteristics, public life, and affairs of local institutions. With their implicit nature, they can be easily mastered by local firms but be unknown to subsidiaries (Henisz and Williamson 1999). These difficulties may intimidate the efforts by international subsidiaries to acquire external knowledge and thus result in a negative moderation on the main relationship.

DISCUSSION AND CONCLUSION

Theoretical Contributions

The findings of our research reflect three major contributions. First, our study fills the gap regarding the role of foreign ownership in EKA. Without taking one of the frequently used theoretical perspectives in international business, such as OLI, our study emphasizes the impact of foreign ownership on firm behavior based on resource dependency theory. We find that, although both types of firms use external sources for their innovation, international subsidiaries tend to rely more on external knowledge due to their liability of foreignness and local adaption. We further show that when an international subsidiary is largely controlled by foreign ownership it appears to acquire more external knowledge for innovation from the local environment. These two findings are supported by resource dependency theory, as the foreign ownership of international subsidiaries requires them to control more external knowledge for innovation to reduce their reliance on the environment, especially those with greater foreign ownership.

Second, our study also contributes to the understanding of the comprehensive moderating effects of institutional hazards on EKA. In prior studies, institutional hazards are considered as a moderator without revealing their complexity (Zaheer 1995; Zaheer and Mosakowski 1997; Luo 2001, 2002). In this study, we have identified two distinct institutional hazards: institution legislation and contract enforcement hazards. Interestingly, they have contrasting moderating effects on the main relationship of this study. Institution legislation hazards positively moderate the relationship between foreign ownership and EKA for innovation. In contrast, contract enforcement hazards have the opposite effects. These contrasting results can be explained by the combination of resource dependency theory and institutional theory under the condition of each hazard.

Third, our findings also contribute to the field of innovation and knowledge management. External knowledge has been recognized as important in the open innovation paradigm. Previously, scholars have focused on the rationale and mechanism for absorbing external knowledge (Calantone and Stanko 2007; Laursen, Masciarelli, and Prencipe 2012; Linder, Jarvenpaa, and Davenport 2003). Our study examines the effects of foreign ownership on EKA for innovation. We find that international subsidiaries and local firms have different levels of preference with regard to knowledge acquisition from external sources. With foreign ownership, international subsidiaries tend to be more active in EKA and, therefore, more energetic with regard to collaborating with local organizations for innovation. However, considering the context of an emerging economy, this relationship is moderated by two types of institutional hazards: institution legislation hazards and contract enforcement hazards. These two types of hazards have contrasting moderating effects and provide a more comprehensive understanding of the behavior of international subsidiaries in terms of EKA.

Practical Implications

The findings of this study have practical implications for managers with responsibility for innovation in emerging countries. First, we emphasize the role of ownership control in the manager's decision regarding the preference for EKA. Managers in international subsidiaries should understand that they would acquire more external knowledge than local firms and, with higher foreign ownership control, international subsidiaries are more likely to acquire external knowledge to increase their local product adaption. Managers should be aware of this request when MNCs have larger ownership control.

Second, with the consideration of institutional hazards in emerging markets, managers should adjust their technology approach to cope with both institution legislation and contract enforcement hazards. When faced with institution legislation hazards, given their foreign ownership, international subsidiaries tend to be more effective and efficient in acquiring external knowledge for innovation. In contrast, when confronted with contract enforcement hazards, subsidiaries are more reluctant to respond to the local market and, thus, less likely to gain external knowledge.

Limitations and Directions for Future Research

The limitations of this study consist of three aspects. First, it focuses on EKA related to product or process innovation, but neglects management innovation from MNCs that cannot be replaced by local knowledge. This extremely superior knowledge can create an attractive environment for international subsidiaries in emerging markets, as the local government gives them priority to conduct local business. Therefore, the relationship suggested in this study may be altered under such a scenario. Second, the findings of this study are based on a cross-sectional sample, which may limit our efforts to demonstrate a causal relationship. Future study may examine the relationship using a longitude dataset. Third, this study used World Bank survey data about China, so the results may not be generalizable to other countries with emerging economies. Further research may address this limitation by using a cross-country dataset to reflect the variations across subsidiaries in different host countries.

NOTE

1. "World to gain from an innovative China." *The Business Times*, July 11, 2011.

FUNDING

This research is supported by the National Natural Science Foundation of China (Grant No. 71772051), and Outstanding Scholar Plan of Fudan University.

REFERENCE

Aiken, L. S., and S. G. West. 1991. *Multiple Regression: Testing and Interpreting Interactions*. Newbury Park, CA: Sage Publications.

Asmussen, C. G. 2009. "Local, Regional, or Global? Quantifying MNE Geographic Scope." *Journal of International Business Studies* 40 (7):1192–205. doi:10.1057/jibs.2008.85.

Back, Y., K. P. Parboteeah, and D. Nam. 2014. "Innovation in Emerging Markets: The Role of Management Consulting Firms." *Journal of International Management* 20 (4):390–405. doi:10.1016/j.intman.2014.07.001.

Barnard, H. 2010. "Overcoming the Liability of Foreignness without Strong Firm Capabilities: The Value of Market-Based Resources." *Journal of International Management* 16 (2):165–76. doi:10.1016/j.intman.2010.03.007.

Barro, R. J. 1991. "Economic Growth in a Cross Section of Countries." *Quarterly Journal of Economics* 106 (2): 407–43. doi:10.2307/2937943.

Bartlett, C. A., and S. Ghoshal. 1989. *Managing across Borders: The Transnational Solution*. Boston, MA: Harvard Business School Press.

Berchicci, L. 2013. "Towards an Open R&D System: Internal R&D Investment, External Knowledge Acquisition and Innovative Performance." *Research Policy* 42 (1):117–27. doi:10.1016/j.respol.2012.04.017.

Boisot, M. H., and J. Child. 1999. "Organizations as Adaptive Systems in Complex Environments: The Case of China." *Organization Science* 10 (3):237–52. doi:10.1287/orsc.10.3.237.

Calantone, R. J., and M. A. Stanko. 2007. "Drivers of Outsourced Innovation: An Exploratory Study." *Journal of Product Innovation Management* 24 (3):230–41. doi:10.1111/j.1540-5885.2007.00247.x.

Cantwell, J. A. 1994. "Introduction." In *Transnational Corporations and Innovatory Activities*, edited by J. A. Cantwell, 1–32. London: Routledge.

Cassiman, B., and R. Veugelers. 2006. "In Search of Complementarity in Innovation Strategy: Internal R&D and External Knowledge Acquisition." *Management Science* 52 (1):68–82. doi:10.1287/mnsc.1050.0470.

Chesbrough, H. W. 2003. *Open Innovation: The New Imperative for Creating and Profiting from Technology.* Boston, MA: Harvard Business School Press.

Chesbrough, H., and A. K. Crowther. 2006. "Beyond High Tech: Early Adopters of Open Innovation in Other Industries." *R and D Management* 36 (3):229–36. doi:10.1111/j.1467-9310.2006.00428.x.

Chesbrough, H. W., and D. J. Teece. 1996. "When Is Virtual Virtuous? Organizing for Innovation." *Harvard Business Review* 74 (1):65–73.

Chesbrough, H. W., W. Vanhaverbeke, and J. West. 2006. *Open Innovation: Researching a New Paradigm.* New York: Oxford University Press, Oxford.

Dehejia, R. H., and S. Wahba. 2002. "Propensity Score-Matching Methods for Nonexperimental Causal Studies." The *Review of Economics and Statistics* 84 (1):151–61. doi:10.1162/003465302317331982.

Deng, P. 2003. "Foreign Direct Investment by Transnationals from Emerging Countries: The Case of China." *Journal of Leadership and Organizational Studies* 10 (2):113–24.

Denk, N., L. Kaufmann., and J.-F. Roesch. 2012. "Liability of Foreignness Revisited: A Review of Contemporary Studies and Recommendations for Future Research." *Journal of International Management* 18 (4):322–34. doi:10.1016/j.intman.2012.07.001.

Dunning, J. H. 1988. "The Eclectic Paradigm of International Production: A Restatement and Some Possible Extensions." *Journal of International Business Studies* 19 (1):1–31. doi:10.1057/palgrave.jibs.8490372.

Elango, B. 2009. "Minimizing Effects of "Liability of Foreignness" Response Strategies of Foreign Firms in the United States." *Journal of World Business* 44 (1):51–62. doi:10.1016/j.jwb.2008.03.012.

Eskridge, William, Jr., P. Frickey, and E. Garrett. 2007. *Legislation and Statutory Interpretation: Concepts and Insights.* 2nd ed. North Carolina: The Carolina Press.

Fan, P. 2006. "Catching up through Developing Innovation Capability: Evidence from China's Telecom-Equipment Industry." *Technovation* 26 (3):359–68. doi:10.1016/j.technovation.2004.10.004.

Feinberg, S., and A. Gupta. 2009. "MNC Subsidiaries and Country Risk: Internalization as a Safeguard against Weak External Institutions." *Academy of Management Journal* 52 (2):381–99. doi:10.5465/amj.2009.37315470.

Gaffney, N., B. Kedia., and J. Clampit. 2013. "A Resource Dependence Perspective of EMNE FDI Strategy." *International Business Review* 22 (6):1092–100. doi:10.1016/j.ibusrev.2013.02.010.

Gao, Y. 2006. "Building *Guanxi* with Government for Foreign Companies in China: A Case Study on the Application of Commitment Instrument." *The Business Review* 6 (2):119–25.

Gao, Y., J. Murray., M. Kotabe, and J. Lu. 2010. "A "Strategy Tripod" Perspective on Export Behaviors: Evidence from Firms Based in an Emerging Economy." *Journal of International Business Studies* 41 (3):377–96. doi:10.1057/jibs.2009.27.

Greif, A. 1993. "Contract Enforceability and Economic Institutions in Early Trade: The Maghribi Traders' Coalition." *American Economic Review* 83 (3):525–48.

Gupta, A. K., and V. Govindarajan. 2000. "Knowledge Flows within the Multinational Corporation." *Strategic Management Journal* 21 (4):473–96. doi:10.1002/(SICI)1097-0266(200004)21:4<473::AID-SMJ84>3.0.CO;2-I.

Henisz, W. J. 2000. "The Institutional Environment for Multinational Investment." *Journal of Law, Economics, and Organization* 16 (2):334–64. doi:10.1093/jleo/16.2.334.

Henisz, W. J., and O. E. Williamson. 1999. "Comparative Economic Organization – within and between Countries." *Business and Politics* 1 (3):261–77. doi:10.1515/bap.1999.1.3.261.

Hillman, A. J., M. C. Wither, and B. J. Collins. 2009. "Resource Dependence Theory: A Review." *Journal of Management* 35 (6):1404–27. doi:10.1177/0149206309343469.

Hitt, M. A., D. Ahlstrom, M. T. Dacin, E. Levitas, and L. Svobodina. 2004. "The Institutional Effects on Strategic Alliance Partner Selection in Transition Economies: China vs. Russia." *Organization Science* 15 (2):173–85. doi:10.1287/orsc.1030.0045.

Hoffman, W. H., and R. Schlosser. 2001. "Success Factors of Strategic Alliances in Small and Medium-Sized Enterprises: An Empirical Survey." *Long Range Planning* 34 (3):357–81. doi:10.1016/S0024-6301(01)00041-3.

Hoskisson, R. E., L. Eden, C. M. Lau, and M. Wright. 2000. "Strategy in Emerging Economies." *Academy of Management Journal* 43 (3):249–67. doi:10.2307/1556394.

Husted, B. W., I. Montiel, and P. Christmann. 2016. "Effects of Local Legitimacy on Certification Decisions to Global and National CSR Standards by Multinational Subsidiaries and Domestic Firms." *Journal of International Business Studies* 47 (3):382–97. doi:10.1057/jibs.2016.3.

Jensen, R., and G. Szulanski. 2004. "Stickiness and the Adaptation of Organizational Practices in Cross-Border Knowledge Transfers." *Journal of International Business Studies* 35 (6):508–23. doi:10.1057/palgrave.jibs.8400107.

Jiang, F., and B. W. Stening. 2013. "Do Indigenous Firms Incur a Liability of Localness When Operating in Their Home Market? The Case of China." *Journal of World Business* 48 (4):478–89. doi:10.1016/j.jwb.2012.09.004.

Johnsen, T. E., W. Phillip, N. Caldwell, and M. Lewis. 2006. "Centrality of Customer and Supplier Interaction in Innovation." *Journal of Business Research* 59 (6):671–8. doi:10.1016/j.jbusres.2005.11.003.

Ju, M., K. Z. Zhou, G. Y. Gao, and J. Lu. 2013. "Technological Capability Growth and Performance Outcome: Foreign versus Local Firms in China." *Journal of International Marketing* 21 (2):1–16. doi:10.1509/jim.12.0171.

Kang, K. H., and J. Kang. 2014. "Do External Knowledge Sourcing Modes Matter for Service Innovation? Empirical Evidence from South Korean Service Firms." *Journal of Product Innovation Management* 31 (1):176–91. doi:10.1111/jpim.12087.

Kraft, M. E. 2007. *Public Policy: Politics, Analysis, and Alternatives.* 2nd ed. Washington, D.C.: Congressional Quarterly, Inc.

Kuemmerle, W. 1997. "Building Effective R&D Capabilities Abroad." *Harvard Business Review* 75 (2):61–70.

Lance, C. E. 1988. "Residual Centering, Exploratory and Confirmatory Moderator Analysis, and Decomposition of Effects in Path Models Containing Interactions." *Applied Psychological Measurement* 12 (2):163–75. doi:10.1177/014662168801200205.

Laursen, K., F. Masciarelli, and A. Prencipe. 2012. "Regions Matter: How Localized Social Capital Affects Innovation and External Knowledge Acquisition." *Organization Science* 23 (1):177–93. doi:10.1287/orsc.1110.0650.

Lawrence, P. L., and J. W. Lorsch. 1967. "Differentiation and Integration in Complex Organizations." *Administrative Science Quarterly* 12 (1):1–47. doi:10.2307/2391211.

Li, J. J., L. Poppo, and K. Z. Zhou. 2008. "Do Managerial Ties in China Always Produce Value? Competition, Uncertainty, and Domestic vs. Foreign Firms." *Strategic Management Journal* 29 (4):383–400. doi:10.1002/smj.665.

Li, J., and J. Zhong. 2003. "Explaining the Growth of International R&D Alliances in China." *Managerial and Decision Economics* 24 (2–3):101–15. doi:10.1002/mde.1079.

Lin, Z., M. K. Peng, H. Yang, and S. L. Sun. 2009. "How Do Networks and Learning Drives M&as? An Institutional Comparison between China and the United States." *Strategic Management Journal* 30 (10):1113–32. doi:10.1002/smj.777.

Linder, J. C., S. Jarvenpaa, and T. H. Davenport. 2003. "Toward an Innovation Sourcing Strategy." *MIT Sloan Management Review* 44 (4):43–49.

Love, J. H., and M. A. Mansury. 2007. "External Linkages, R&D and Innovation Performance in US Business Services." *Industry & Innovation* 14 (5):477–96. doi:10.1080/13662710701711380.

Luo, Y. 2001. "Determinants of Local Responsiveness: Perspectives from Foreign Subsidiaries in an Emerging Market." *Journal of Management* 27 (4):451–77. doi:10.1177/014920630102700404.

Luo, Y. 2002. "Contract, Cooperation, and Performance in International Joint Ventures." *Strategic Management Journal* 23 (10):903–19. doi:10.1002/smj.261.

Luo, Y. 2003. "Market-Seeking MNEs in an Emerging Market: How Parent-Subsidiary Links Shape Overseas Success." *Journal of International Business Studies* 34 (3):290–309. doi:10.1057/palgrave.jibs.8400027.

Marshall, A. 1890. *Principles of Economics.* 1st ed. London: Macmillan and Co.

Meyer, K. E., R. Mudambi, and R. Narula. 2011. "Multinational Enterprises and Local Contexts: The Opportunities and Challenges of Multiple Embeddedness." *Journal of Management Studies* 48 (2):235–52.

Mohr, J., and R. Spekman. 1994. "Characteristics of Partnership Success: Partnership Attributes, Communication Behavior, and Conflict Resolution Techniques." *Strategic Management Journal* 15 (2):135–52. doi:10.1002/smj.4250150205.

Mudambi, R. 2011. "Hierarchy, Coordination, and Innovation in the Multinational Enterprise." *Global Strategy Journal* 1 (3–4):317–23. doi:10.1002/gsj.32.

Nohria, N., and S. Ghoshal. 1997. *The Differentiated Network: Organizing Multinational Corporations for Value Creation*. San Francisco, CA: Jossey-Bass Publishers.

Nolan, P. 2001. *China and the Global Business Revolution*. Houndsmill: Palgrave.

North, D. C. 1981. *Structure and Change in Economic History*. New York: Norton.

North, D. C. 1990. *Institutions, Institutional Change and Economic Performance*. Cambridge, MA: Harvard University Press.

North, D. C., and R. P. Thomas. 1973. *The Rise of the Western World*. Cambridge: Cambridge University Press.

Pearce, R. D. 1999. "Decentralized R&D and Strategic Competitiveness: Globalized Approaches to Generation and Use of Technology in Multinational Enterprises (MNEs)." *Research Policy* 28 (2–3):157–78. doi:10.1016/S0048-7333(98)00115-2.

Peng, M. W., and Y. Luo. 2000. "Managerial Ties and Firm Performance in a Transition Economy: The Nature of a Micro-Macro Link." *Academy of Management Journal* 43 (3):486–501. doi:10.2307/1556406.

Peng, M. W., D. Wang, and Y. Jiang. 2008. "An Institution-Based View of International Business Strategy: A Focus on Emerging Economies." *Journal of International Business Studies* 39 (5):920–36. doi:10.1057/palgrave.jibs.8400377.

Pfeffer, J., and G. R. Salancik. 1978. *The External Control of Organizations: A Resource Dependence Perspective*. New York: Harper & Row.

Podolny, J. M., and K. L. Page. 1998. "Network Forms of Organization." *Annual Review of Sociology* 24 (1):57–76. doi:10.1146/annurev.soc.24.1.57.

Rothaermel, F. T. 2001. "Incumbent's Advantage through Exploiting Complementary Assets via Interfirm Cooperation." *Strategic Management Journal* 22 (6–7):687–99. doi:10.1002/smj.180.

Rangan, S., and A. Drummond. 2004. "Explaining Outcomes in Competition among Foreign Multinationals in a Focal Host Market." *Strategic Management Journal* 25 (3):285–93. doi:10.1002/smj.375.

Ren, S., A. B. Eisingerich, and H. Tsai. 2014. "Search Scope and Innovation Performance of Emerging-Market Firms." *Journal of Business Research* 68 (1):102–8. doi:10.1016/j.jbusres.2014.04.011.

Rigby, D., and C. Zook. 2002. " Open-market Innovation." *Harvard Business Review* 80 (10):80–89.

Saliola, F., and A. Zanfei. 2009. "Multinational Firms, Global Value Chains and the Organization of Knowledge Transfer." *Research Policy* 38 (2):369–81. doi:10.1016/j.respol.2008.11.003.

Scott, W. R. 2004. "Institutional Theory." In *Encyclopedia of Social Theory*, edited by G. Ritzer, 408–14. Thousand Oaks, CA: Sage.

Sheth, J. N. 2011. "Impact of Emerging Markets on Marketing: Rethinking Existing Perspectives and Practices." *Journal of Marketing* 75 (4):166–82. doi:10.1509/jmkg.75.4.166.

Shleifer, A., and R. W. Vishny. 1997. "The Limits of Arbitrage." *Journal of Finance* 52 (1):35–55. doi:10.1111/j.1540-6261.1997.tb03807.x.

Short, H. 1994. "Ownership, Control, Financial Structure and the Performance of Firms." *Journal of Economic Surveys* 8 (3):203–49. doi:10.1111/j.1467-6419.1994.tb00102.x.

Srholec, M. A. 2011. "Multilevel Analysis of Innovation in Developing Countries." *Industrial and Corporate Change* 20 (6):1539–69. doi:10.1093/icc/dtr024.

Uhlenbruck, K., P. Rodriguez, J. Doh, and L. Eden. 2006. "The Impact of Corruption on Entry Strategy: Evidence from Telecommunication Projects in Emerging Economies." *Organization Science* 17 (3):402–14. doi:10.1287/orsc.1060.0186.

Warner, M., N. S. Hong, and X. Xu. 2004. "Late Development Experience and the Evolution of Transnational Firms in the People's Republic Of China." *Asia Pacific Business Review* 10 (3–4):324–45. doi:10.1080/1360238042000264397.

Wu, J. 2013. "Diverse Institutional Environment and Product Innovation of Emerging Market Firms." *Management International Review* 53 (1):39–59. doi:10.1007/s11575-012-0162-z.

Wu, J., and Z. Wu. 2014. "Integrated Risk Management and Product Innovation in China: The Moderating Role of Board of Directors." *Technovation* 34 (8):466–76. doi:10.1016/j.technovation.2013.11.006.

Van de Vrande, V. C. Lemmens, and W. Vanhaverbeke. 2006. "Choosing Governance Modes for External Technology Sourcing." *R and D Management* 36 (3):347–63. doi:10.1111/j.1467-9310.2006.00434.x.

Yan, A., and B. Gray. 1994. "Bargaining Power, Management Control, and Performance in US – China Joint Ventures: A Comparative Case Study." *Academy of Management Journal* 37 (6):1478–517. doi:10.2307/256796.

Zaheer, S. 1995. "Overcoming the Liability of Foreignness." *Academy of Management Journal* 38 (2):341–64. doi: 10.2307/256683.

Zaheer, S., and E. Mosakowski. 1997. "The Dynamics of the Liability of Foreignness: A Global Study of Survival in Financial Services." *Strategic Management Journal* 18 (6):439–463.

Zhang, Y. 2003. *China's Emerging Global Businesses: Political Economy and Institutional Investigations.* Basingstoke: Palgrave Macmillan.

Zhang, Y., H. Li, and M. A. Hitt. 2007. "R&D Intensity and International Joint Venture Performance in an Emerging Market: Moderating Effects of Market Focus and Ownership Structure." *Journal of International Business Studies* 38 (6):944–60. doi:10.1057/palgrave.jibs.8400301.

How Does Competition By Informal Firms Affect The Innovation In Formal Firms?

Jorge Heredia Perez, Xiaohua Yang, Ou Bai, Alejandro Flores and
Walter Heredia Heredia

Abstract: This study applies a resource-based perspective to investigate how competition by informal firms affects innovation in formal firms in China. By analyzing survey data, collected from 1,686 Chinese manufacturing firms, we find that formal firms tend to increase their rate of innovation when faced with informal competition. However, formal firms' access to increased global supply chain collaboration mitigates the challenges presented to their rate of innovation by the informal firms. We present implications for future research, practice, and policy-making.

Innovation has been regarded as a key driver for Chinese economic growth (Wang et al. 2008). In fact, to keep a 5.5 to 6.5 percent economic growth rate for the next decade, China will need national innovation to generate a 2 to 3 percent increase in annual gross domestic product (GDP) to achieve its goals. Recently, "Mass Entrepreneurship and Innovation by All" (大众创业万众创新) has become national policy for economic transition and transformation (Shen 2016). Formal Chinese firms are part of this national strategy and are encouraged to pursue innovation at home and abroad. How effective they have been pursuing innovation has recently become of interest to scholars (Lee and Hung 2014; Ren and Yu 2016; Wang, Cooke, and Lin 2016).

However, competition by informal firms has become a significant strategic concern for formal firms and may interfere with formal firms' innovation strategy (Mccann and Bahl 2016). Informal firms, unlike formal firms, are firms that may not be registered and do operate outside of government regulation and taxation systems (Webb et al. 2013). Although existing research has generated much knowledge in this area, much of it was conducted in the context of developed economies. Emerging economies have different social, political, and economic contexts and different firm characteristics than in developed economies. The competitive behaviors of formal firms facing the competition by informal firms in emerging economies have rarely been examined (McGahan 2012; Darbi, Hall, and Knott 2018; Iriyama, Kishore, and Talukdar 2016; Mccann and Bahl 2016; Mendi and Costamagna 2017).

Informal firms account for an increasingly and significantly larger economic proportion of total number of firms in emerging economies. Schneider (2002) suggests that the informal sector generates 40 percent of the GDP in emerging economies. The informal economy is defined as economic activities in the production and trade of goods and services that are conducted by informal firms operating outside of government regulation and taxation systems (Webb et al. 2013). In fact, the China 2012 World Bank survey[1] shows that 57.7 percent of formal firms compete with informal firms. Thus, in the case of Shan-Zhai[2], the informal firms mobile phones adapted their products to the domestic market, achieved great success, and were accepted by Chinese customers (Lee and Hung 2014; Williams and Martinez-Perez 2014). Therefore, we have chosen to examine China's institutional context to study the relationship between competition by informal firms and the rate of innovation in formal firms (Li and Atuahene-Gima 2001; Hoskisson et al. 2013; Liu 2017).

This study examines how informal firms' competition affects the innovation in formal firms in China. While innovation may be a response to the competition by informal firms, the existing literature about the effect of competition by informal firms on formal firms' innovation is inconclusive (Mccann and Bahl 2016; Mendi and Costamagna 2017). Therefore, this study investigates what kinds of resources and capacity moderate the relationships between informal competition and the innovation in formal firms. We employ and analyze data to empirically address these questions in the national context of newly developed emerging economies such as China (Hoskisson et al. 2013).

Our findings confirm that informal firms' competition has a positive effect on the rate of innovation in Chinese formal firms. However, the positive effect decreases when formal firms have high levels of supply chain collaborative capabilities (Cao and Zhang 2011). Global supply chain collaboration is a valuable, rare, organizational, and inimitable resource developed by formal firms to improve the trust and long-term relationships with their partners in the value chain.

Supply chain collaboration enables formal firms to work with their clients at a fast speed, thus increasing customers' retention as a strategic resource for the firms' competitive advantage (Soosay, Hyland, and Ferrer 2008; Kunc and Morecroft 2010; Cao and Zhang 2011; Ramanathan and Gunasekaran 2014). Additionally, supply chain collaboration reduces the bullwhip effect. Bullwhip refers to increasing swings in inventory in response to shifts in customers' demand as one moves further up the supply chain. The bullwhip effect is a typical problem produced by the inadequate administration of the inventories (raw materials, products in process, or finished products), uncertainty, radical management turnover, and inaccurate demand forecasts, which increase costs and decrease operational performance for formal firms (Shan et al. 2014; Zawawi, Wahab, and Mamun 2017).

Our study contributes to the resource-based view (RBV) theory in two ways. First, it confirms that informal competition is a significant force that increases innovation of formal firms in developing economies, such as China. Innovation becomes a critical resource for formal firms to counter the pressure of informal competition. Second, our work offers an essential extension to RBV by demonstrating how the supply chain collaboration of formal firms affects the relationship between informal competition and innovation. Our findings show that supply chain collaboration is a strategic resource. Indeed, supply chain collaboration provides a new kind of capability for formal firms when they compete with informal firms.

The article is structured as follows. In the next section, the theoretical framework and hypotheses are developed. Section three describes the methodology. Section four presents the empirical test analysis and results. Finally, we discuss our theoretical contribution, practical implications, limitations, and future research in section five.

THEORY AND HYPOTHESES

We draw upon the RBV to study formal firms' competition behaviors in emerging economies (Hoskisson et al. 2000). We build upon Barney's (1996) study that describes the impact of strategic resources and available capabilities of a firm on its performance. A firm can achieve competitive advantages when it can exploit advantageous resources (Barney 2001). RBV suggests that firms compete for strategic resources to achieve competitive advantages and provide value to the clients. Our research applies RBV to investigate and explain the relationships between the competition by informal firms and the innovation of formal firms in China. Additionally, we investigate how formal firms' capabilities (i.e., supply chain collaboration) moderate this relationship in a country context specific to China's newly developed emerging economy. The conceptual model is shown in Figure 1.

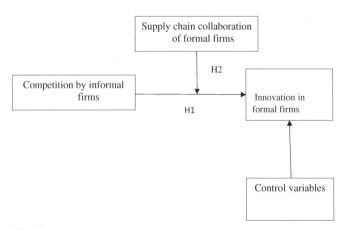

FIGURE 1. Proposed Model

Competition from Informal Firms in New Developed Emerging Economies

From the perspective of RBV, formal and informal firms compete for strategic resources, such as products, customers, and human capital (McGahan 2012; Distinguin, Rugemintwari, and Tacneng 2016; Mendi and Costamagna 2017). Formal firms identify informal firms as direct competition since they serve the same market and exploit similar resources. Formal firms perceive informal firms as market share captors with advantages in costs and flexibility of products and processes (Williams and Martinez-Perez 2014; Mendi and Costamagna 2017).

Following the resource-based view, formal firms must develop new strategic resources and capabilities, such as innovation, to differentiate themselves from the informal competition. Differentiation from informal firms allows formal firms to increase customers' loyalty and the value of the product to attract customers. This strategy has the potential to obtain and sustain competitive advantage (Williams and Martinez-Perez 2014; Kunc and Morecroft 2009).

The institutional context is a relevant external factor for the formal firms' innovation. China has achieved great progress in the development of institutions (i.e., IPR) and market's structures (Hoskisson et al. 2013; Peng 2013; Liu 2017). China has also accumulated R&D capabilities and resources for innovation in recent years (Liu 2017). The Chinese government has made significant efforts to create a sustainable innovation system and has made substantial investments in engineers training (Liu 2017). These national contexts can be considered as new external resources accessible to formal firms because these firms have more legitimacy (market acceptance by playing according the rules of the games) than informal firms (Deephouse 1999). Then, formal firms have more resources for innovation that allow them to better compete with informal firms.

Informal competition is a major force in China. Informal firms in China have qualified staff with university degrees (Hoskisson et al. 2013; Ahlstrom and Ding 2014; Lee and Hung 2014; Wang, Cooke, and Lin 2016). University undergraduates choose informal firms as their first job to obtain experience (Wang, Cooke, and Lin 2016). These informal firms reach customers through e-commerce channels, such as alibabab.com, and offer a great variety of products with specific characteristics in each region of China (Lee and Hung 2014).

In the context of this competitive dynamic, formal firms face direct competition by informal firms since they both use similar resources and serve the same market. They risk diminishing competitive advantages as a result of low-cost and low-priced products and services supplied by informal firms and consumed by custumers. Therefore, formal firms need to implement innovation activities to provide differentiated products to Chinese customers, who demand products with more functionality and reasonably priced, when they are facing competition by informal firms (Mccann and Bahl 2016).

Under the "indigenous innovation" strategy in China (Wang et al. 2008), formal firms create innovative knowledge by embracing market needs and answering to characteristics unique to Chinese customers. In addition, they have strong support from the Chinese government to engage in innovation activities (Liu 2017). Thus, we hypothesize as follows:

H1: The competition from informal firms is positively related to formal firms' innovation.

The Moderating Effect of Supply Chain Collaboration on the Relationship between Informal Firms' Competition and Formal Firms' Innovation

Mendi and Costamagna (2017) found that the competition by informal firms discouraged formal firms from introducing new products or processes. However, Mccann and Bahl (2016) suggest, based on their study, that competition from informal firms encourages formal firms to introduce innovation in manufacturing firms. Given the inconsistent findings, we argue that the relationship between informal firms and formal firms may not be linear and it may be moderated by some specific firms' resources, as Parnell (2011) indicated.

In the case of China, there is an increase in outsourcing over the last two decades, increase in concentration and globalization of retailing, flux of international circulation of talents and professional services, codification of knowledge, and the increasingly open market for corporate control in multi-countries. All these business chracterics triggered modularization of global value chains that made it more attractive to Chinese formal firms to participate in global value chains collaboration (Williamson and Zeng 2009; Zawawi, Wahab, and Mamun 2017).

Among the different resources, supply chain collaboration is garnering increasing importance in shaping the innovation behavior and strategies in formal firms, given that supply chain collaboration allows formal firms to reduce the bullwhip effect (Shan et al. 2014; Zawawi, Wahab, and Mamun 2017). Hence, supply chain collaboration is considered to be a crucial resource for developing core competencies in formal Chinese firms (Khan, Rao-Nicholson, and Tarba 2018). Specifically, supply chain collaboration allows formal firms to share information with suppliers and clients, including demand forecasts, production plans, inventories, and the replenishment of products at the point of sale (Soosay, Hyland, and Ferrer 2008). Therefore, supply chain collaboration enables formal firms to counter the pressure exerts by the informal firms' competition.

First, supply chain collaboration allows formal firms to capture strategic market resources, such as clients, and external resources, such as government support. Thus, the supply chain collaboration gives the formal firms greater flexibility to meet its customers' requirements (Desarbo et al. 2005; Soosay, Hyland, and Ferrer 2008; Cao and Zhang 2011; Ramanathan and Gunasekaran 2014). Second, supply chain collaboration allows formal firms to develop long-term relationships with their suppliers, which may provide strategic resources for innovation (Soosay, Hyland, and Ferrer 2008; Khan, Rao-Nicholson, and Tarba 2018). Therefore, formal firms could be differentiated and hence generate more value for customers than informal firms.

Thus, supply chain collaboration increases the barriers to imitation and differentiates and reduces the competition introduced by informal firms (Reed and DeFillippi 1990; Kunc and Morecroft 2010). Therefore, supply chain collaboration is a strategic resource for formal firms that is difficult for informal firms to acquire since the government does not legitimize informal firms (Lee and Hung 2014; Ren, Yu, and Zhu 2016). They cannot enter the global market because they do not have access to the network of contacts given and permits issued by the government (Lee and Hung 2014; Ren and Yu 2016). Therefore, formal firms can take advantage of the benefits provided by the government and improve their supply chain collaboration. Formal firms do not see informal firms as direct competitors since formal firms can compete and sell their products in the global market (Lee and Hung 2014; Ren and Yu 2016).Thus, we hypothesize as follows:

> H2: The level of supply chain collaboration moderates the relationship between the competition by informal firms and innovation in formal firms.

METHODS

Sample

We focus on manufacturing industries because investments in innovation in manufacturing are far more significant compared to other industrial sectors, such as services or nonprofits (Allred and Park 2007). Moreover, innovation is relatively more important in manufacturing, where knowledge and skills are valued (Crespi and Zuniga 2012). Table 1 shows the descriptive statistics. It provides a detailed list of innovation activities' (product, process, or both) and status and expenditures on innovation (a percentage of total turnover from innovation) in Chinese manufacturing firms. Table 1 indicates that approximately 65% of companies in the manufacturing sector engage in innovation. The percentage of internal R&D expenditures is approximately 6.08%.

To test the hypotheses, we employed data from the 2012 World Bank's Enterprise Survey of 1,686 manufacturing firms in China. The survey provides information about the companies' characteristics, strategies, and economic performance, their perceptions of the institutional, policy, and economic environments, and the degree of competition at which they operate[3]. China provides an interesting context for our analysis. First, China has a unique institutional context where the informal sector plays an important role in the labor market. The economic reforms not only gave rise to double-digit economic growth for a couple of decades, but it also gave rise to the informal sector in China. China's informal employment

TABLE 1
Descriptive Statistics for the Main Variables

Number of observations	1,686
Innovation activities (as % of total firms):	65%
Expenditure on innovation by type (as a % of total turnover of innovation)	
R&D internal	6.08%
Share of firms that performed R&D internal	41.28%
Share of turnover from product innovations (as a % of total turnover)	12.98%
Human Resource (as a % of total permanent workers in sector)	
Share of workers with secondary school	17.22%
Share of firms that cooperation with other enterprises or science and technology institutions	40.56%
Total sales (MM-US dollar)[1]	54,400

[1]Exchange rate for the year 2012.

Source: Enterprise Survey's World Bank of China.

Own Elaboration.

consists of an average of 30.1 million self-employed persons, as well as 98.6 million persons who work in informal firms (Huang 2009).

China is a BRIC country (which refers to the countries of Brazil, Russia, India, and China) with a different environment than traditional emerging markets (Reed and DeFillippi 1990; Cui, Jiao, and Jiao 2016). China belongs to a new category of economies called newly developed emerging economies. These economies have adequately developed market institutions and the necessary economic infrastructure to facilitate high level of R&D investment and developmental capabilities for innovation (Becheikh, Landry, and Amara 2006; Hoskisson et al. 2013).

Our data are from the Enterprise Survey that has been used in some prior published studies (Distinguin, Rugemintwari, and Tacneng 2016; Iriyama, Kishore, and Talukdar 2016; Mccann and Bahl 2016; Mendi and Costamagna 2017). The data are suitable for studying the phenomenon of competition by informal firms.

Measurement of Variables

Table 2 provides a detailed summary of the operationalization of each variable in the theoretical model proposed in Figure 1.

Dependent Variable

Following the OECD/Eurostat (2005), we define innovation as the ability of the organization to offer or implement a new or significantly improved product (good or service). We measure innovation type by using the operationalized new product development (NPD) variable, using data from the question of the survey that assigns the value of (1) if any new products or services were introduced during the last three years and (0) otherwise; this represents some level of firms' innovations (Mccann and Bahl 2016; Mendi and Costamagna 2017).

Independent Variable

We measure competition by informal firms using the question about the extent to which competitors in the informal sectors are an obstacle to the current operations of the formal firms. The question used on a 5-point Likert scale: no (0), minor (1), moderate (2), major (3), and very severe obstacle (4) (Iriyama, Kishore, and Talukdar 2016; Mccann and Bahl 2016; Mendi and Costamagna 2017). With the objective of reducing the respondent's subjective perceptions about the intensity of competition, we measure the average of the informal competition by region (Mccann and Bahl 2016; Mendi and Costamagna 2017). Thus, we assume that responding managers in each region confront similar intense competition from informal firms (Mccann and Bahl 2016; Mendi and Costamagna 2017). Following Huang (2017), we choose a region as our measure of the refrence group because the level of the informal economy is influenced predominantly by the conditions in each region in China.

TABLE 2
Variables Definition

Category	Sub-Category (Country)	Item-Description	Variables	References
Dependent	Innovation (New Product Development)	Takes value one if the firm introduced a new process or service, 0 otherwise	Dichotomous	Becheikh, Landry, and Amara (2006); Geldes et al. (2017); Mccann and Bahl (2016); Mendi and Costamagna (2017)
Independent	Informal competition	Regional average of informal firms as obstacle to firm's operations	Numerical	Distinguin et al. (2016); Gonzalez and Lamanna (2007); Iriyama, Kishore, and Talukdar (2016); Mccann and Bahl (2016); Mendi and Costamagna (2017)
Control	Age	Log of year of operations	Numerical	Becheikh, Landry, and Amara (2006); Geldes et al. (2017); Mccann and Bahl (2016); Mendi and Costamagna, (2017); Zhang, Sarker, and Sarker (2008)
	Size	Log of full-time individuals workers	Numerical	
	Government owner	Percentage of this firm is owned by Government or State	Numerical	
	Private foreign	Percentage of this firm is owned by Private foreign individuals, companies or organizations.	Numerical	
	Direct export	Percentage of this establishment's sales were: Direct exports	Numerical	
	Internet to R&D	Internet connection to do research and develop ideas	Dichotomous	
	Skill prod worker	Log number of skilled production workers	Numerical	
	Manager experience	Log top manager years of experience	Numerical	
	Years education	Years of education of typical production worker	Numerical	
	Cooperation suppliers	Introduced new products or services: Developed in cooperation with suppliers	Dichotomous	
	Cooperation clients	Introduced new products or services: Developed in cooperation with client firms	Dichotomous	
	Pursued contracts from government	Has this establishment secured or attempted to secure a government contract	Dichotomous	
	Formal competition	Number of competitors did this establishment's main product face	Numerical	
Moderator	Supply chain collaboration	Sharing production and replenishment plans with clients	Numerical	Cao and Zhang (2011); Ramanathan and Gunasekaran (2014); Soosay, Hyland, and Ferrer (2008)
		Sharing raw material inventory with raw material suppliers		
		Sharing finished goods inventory with clients		

Own Elaboration from the World Bank Enterprise Survey.

Moderator Variable

Following Ramanathan and Gunasekaran (2014), we use the supply chain collaboration measurement using three items from the survey: (1) sharing production and replenishment plans; (2) raw material inventory with suppliers; and (3) finished goods inventory with clients. The survey reported a dummy variable for each of the three questions. We perform the polychoric STATA command option of a factor analysis, and then we utilize the varimax rotation to find an orthogonal factor. Finally, we use the command prediction to create a factor supply chain collaboration variable as an antecedent of NPD. The measurement of supply chain collaboration satisfies the convergent validity (AVE = 0.5 and CR = 0.73).

Control Variables

We control for industry fixed effects to reduce variation between industries. Additionally, because innovation may vary based on other firm's characteristics, we control for size, age, export orientation, and ownership (Becheikh, Landry, and Amara 2006; Byrne 2010; Mccann and Bahl 2016; Mendi and Costamagna 2017). To control for size and age effects, we use the log of the number of full-time employees and the log of the years of operation. To control for export orientation, we consider a numerical variable that categorizes the firms' percentage of sales that are direct exports. We also include resources and technological capabilities, such as availability of internet, research and development, manager experience, managers' years of education, and cooperation (Mccann and Bahl 2016; Mendi and Costamagna 2017; Zhang, Sarker, and Sarker 2008). Additionally, we consider other control variables that are related to innovation, such as pursued contracts from the government (Soosay, Hyland, and Ferrer 2008; Mccann and Bahl 2016). Finally, we control the important control variable of formal competition by considering the number of competitors the formal firm faces in a specific product (Mendi and Costamagna 2017).

Model Specification

The dependent variable of the study, namely innovation, is dichotomous. It requires the use of logistic regression (Geldes and Felzensztein 2013; Geldes, Felzensztein, and Palacios-Fenech 2017). However, we see that our dataset has more than one variable with missing values. To reduce the loss of observations and recover the information for the missing values, we apply the multivariate imputation command. Because the missing values are at random, we can consider using the suite of -mi- commands for Multiple Imputation (MI) (Royston 2004). For the multivariate imputation of a combination of continues and binary scales used in the various variables that combine innovate, we use the -mi impute chained- commands. The procedure has two steps: First, recover the information from the variables with missing values using the -mi impute chained- commands. Second, perform the logistic regression model using the "mi estimate-command" in the STATA 13 statistical package (Royston 2004).

RESULTS

Table 3 shows summary of the descriptive statistics and pairwise correlations of the variables used in the logit analysis. For each variable, we reported its average, standard deviation, and minimum and maximum values. In our sample, most firms are medium size enterprises. Fifty percent of firms in our sample have introduced an innovation. The score for the average value of competitive pressure from companies in the informal sector is 0.83.

Table 4 displays the logit regression of each hypothesis. It indicates that formal firms in China increased innovation activities when faced with informal competition. In the first column, model 0 that contains only the control variables is the baseline model for innovation. In model 1, we found a positive relationship between informal competition and innovation strategy ($b = 1.41$, $p < 0.01$). Thus, Hypothesis 1 is supported. Additionally, the results of Table 4 in model 2 show the interaction between supply chain collaboration and informal competition ($b = -0.74$, $p < 0.10$). The relationship between informal competition and innovation weakened when the firm developed supply chain collaboration. Thus, Hypothesis 2 is also supported.

Robustness

For the robustness test, we consider an alternative form of the dependent variable. More specifically, we use the survey question that assessed if the establishment spent money on research and development activities within the facility. We verify that results are similar; informal competition has a positive effect and is significant ($b = 1.29$; $p < 0.01$). See Table 5.

DISCUSSIONS AND CONCLUSIONS

Context matters (Yang and Terjesen 2007). This study provides an extension to the resource-based view with our explanations of how informal competition affects the innovation of formal firms in the unique context of China. Our findings suggest that study of firms' innovation behavior and strategies needs to take account of their domestic context as well as their international strategies. Our study contributes to RBV in two ways. First, we extend the RBV as the valid theory to explain how formal firms deal with informal firms, in a context of newly developed emerging economies, such as China (Barney 2001). Our work confirms that informal competition is a significant force driving innovation of formal firms in China. Innovation becomes an answer for formal firms to develop valuable, unique products and services (vis-à-vis Shan-Zhai products) to counter the pressure of informal competition at home. Second, our work offers an important extension to RBV by demonstrating how the global supply chain collaboration can become valuable, unique, and not so easily imitable resource for formal firms to leverage and to compete with domestic informal firms and, thus, to mitigate the expensive investment in innovation.

Our findings are consistent with previous research, such as Mccann and Bahl's (2016) who found that the competition from informal firms has a positive effect on NPD. More

TABLE 3
Descriptive Statistics

Variable	Obs	Mean	Std.	Min	Max	1	2	3	4	5	6	7	8	9	10	11	12	13	14	15	16
1. New Product Development	1680	0.46	0.50	0.00	1.00	1.00															
2. Age	1645	2.43	0.52	0.00	4.83	0.04*	1.00														
3. Size	1643	4.26	1.31	1.10	10.24	0.15***	0.21***	1.00													
4. Government owner	1683	3.42	16.63	0.00	95.00	−0.13***	0.03	0.04	1.00												
5. Private foreign owner	1683	4.75	18.81	0.00	100.00	0.05*	−0.06**	0.05**	−0.05**	1.00											
6. Direct export	1685	9.10	22.47	0.00	100.00	0.05*	−0.03	0.19***	−0.06**	0.19***	1.00										
7. Internet to R&D	1657	0.59	0.49	0.00	1.00	0.28***	0.06**	0.21***	0.06**	0.03	0.08***	1.00									
8. Skill workers	1661	3.18	1.40	0.00	9.31	0.16***	0.17***	0.85***	0.12***	0.04*	0.17***	0.25***	1.00								
9. Manager experience	1659	2.72	0.49	0.00	3.85	0.07***	0.36***	0.17***	−0.10***	−0.03	0.07*	0.04*	0.16***	1.00							
10. Years education	1649	10.18	1.88	1.00	18.00	0.06**	0.04	0.04	−0.04	0.04	0.05**	0.08***	0.03	0.04	1.00						
11. Cooperation suppliers	1466	0.28	0.45	0.00	1.00	0.13***	−0.03	0.08***	−0.13***	0.04	0.04	0.12***	0.02	−0.03	0.00	1.00					
12. Cooperation clients	1466	0.37	0.48	0.00	1.00	0.19***	−0.01	0.06**	−0.12***	0.08***	0.04	0.14***	0.03	0.01	−0.06**	0.53***	1.00				
13. Pursued contracts from government	1659	0.12	0.32	0.00	1.00	0.12***	0.01	0.17***	−0.05*	0.01	0.04*	0.09***	0.15***	0.06**	0.07***	0.07**	0.09***	1.00			
14. Formal competition	217	15.51	40.66	0.00	500.00	−0.07	−0.13*	−0.06	0.16**	−0.05	−0.08	−0.12*	−0.12*	−0.26***	−0.04	0.11	−0.03	−0.03	1.00		
15. Supply chain collaboration	1651	0.44	0.41	0	1.01	0.21***	0.03	0.15***	−0.11***	−0.0068	0.05***	0.12***	0.13***	0.11***	0.03	0.30***	0.27***	0.09***	0.09	1.00	
16. Informal competition	1686	0.83	0.37	0.30	2.04	0.21***	0.04*	0.01	−0.18***	0.05*	−0.02	0.03	0.07**	0.08***	−0.17***	0.09***	0.07***	−0.06**	−0.13*	0.08***	1.00

Significance at $*p < 0.10$; $**p < 0.05$; $***p < 0.01$.

TABLE 4
Logistic Regression Analyses

Variables	Model 0 New Product Development	Model 1 New Product Development	Model 2 New Product Development
Age	−0.02	−0.04	−0.04
	(0.12)	(0.12)	(0.12)
Size	0.03	−0.05	−0.05
	(0.08)	(0.09)	(0.09)
Government owner	−0.02***	−0.02***	−0.02***
	(0.01)	(0.01)	(0.01)
Private foreign	0.00	0.00	0.00
	(0.00)	(0.00)	(0.00)
Direct export	0.00	0.00	0.00
	(0.00)	(0.00)	(0.00)
Internet to R&D	0.96***	0.94***	0.95***
	(0.12)	(0.12)	(0.12)
Skill workers	0.12	0.23**	0.23**
	(0.08)	(0.08)	(0.08)
Manager experience	0.08	0.05	0.05
	(0.13)	(0.14)	(0.14)
Years education	0.03	0.08**	0.08**
	(0.03)	(0.03)	(0.03)
Cooperation with suppliers	−0.05	−0.15	−0.1
	(0.16)	(0.16)	(0.16)
Cooperation with clients	0.53***	0.60***	0.58***
	(0.14)	(0.14)	(0.14)
Pursued contracts from government	0.46**	0.60***	0.62***
	(0.18)	(0.18)	(0.18)
Formal competition	0.00	0.000	0.00
	(0.00)	(0.00)	(0.00)
Supply chain collaboration	0.71***	0.69***	1.30***
	(0.14)	(0.15)	(0.38)
Informal competition		1.41***	1.71***
		(0.17)	(0.25)
Informal competition × supply chain collaboration			−0.74*
			(0.43)
Industry fixed effects	YES	YES	YES
Wald Chi-squared	13.33***	14.89***	14.22***
Number of observations	1673	1673	1673

Dependent variable: New or upgraded product/service (yes = 1, no = 0).
Standard errors in parentheses; $p^{***} < 0.01$; $p^{**} < 0.05$; $p^{*} < 0.10$.

interestingly, we find this positive effect to decrease when formal firms develop the capability for supply chain collaboration. In this case, the supply chain collaboration is leveraged as a competitive advantage and as a vehicle to coordinate and strengthen the relationships with principal partners, such as clients, suppliers, and contractors. Therefore, our findings confirm that firms can become competitive and successful if they focus on developing core competencies, such as supply chain collaboration that is unique, valuable, and not easily imitable (Barney 1996).

TABLE 5
Logistic Regression Analyses to Robustness Test

	R&D Activities
Age	−0.18
	(0.12)
Size	0.24***
	(0.09)
Government owner	−0.02***
	(0.01)
Private foreign	0.00
	(0.00)
Direct export	0.00
	(0.00)
Internet to R&D	1.03***
	(0.13)
Skill workers	0.03
	(0.08)
Manager experience	0.43***
	(0.14)
Years education	0.13***
	(0.03)
Cooperation with suppliers	−0.06
	(0.16)
Cooperation with clients	0.10
	(0.15)
Pursued contracts from government	0.37**
	(0.18)
Formal competition	0.00
	(0.00)
Supply chain collaboration	0.47***
	(0.15)
Informal competition	1.29***
	(0.17)
Industry fixed effects	YES
Wald Chi-squared	14.92***
Number of observations	1,669

Dependent variable: R&D activities (yes = 1, no = 0).
Standard errors in parentheses; $p^{***} < 0.01$; $p^{**} < 0.05$; $p^{*} < 0.10$.

Legitimate formal firms that play by the rules of the games at home can be shielded from the competition by informal firms at home if they can strategically participate in global value chain collaboration and leverage it again competition from informal firms (Soosay, Hyland, and Ferrer 2008; Cao and Zhang 2011; Ramanathan and Gunasekaran 2014). Also, formal firms' supply chain collaboration allows them to reduce the bullwhip effect, a competitive weapon that domestic informal firms do not possess. These superior supply chain collaboration capabilities enable the formal firm to balance the strategy to counter the informal firms' competition and increase the strategic attention on the collaboration with other MNEs to provide more significant value to the customer (Deephouse 1999; Khan, Rao-Nicholson, and Tarba 2018).

LIMITATIONS

We are aware of the limitations of this study. First, this study is context-specific, as it focuses solely on Chinese firms. Due to the vast differences between China and other emerging economies, the generalizability of our conclusions may be limited. Therefore, applicability to another context must be validated.

Second, the cross-sectional nature of the research into a dynamic concept enables the analysis of the organizations' situations at only one specific point in time. Future research should consider performing analysis using panel data or other longitudinal data.

Third, the dependent variable only captures the activities belonging to product innovation. However, it could be interesting to evaluate the effect of informal firms' competition in non-technological innovations (organizational and marketing).

Furthermore, future research could explore the role of informal competition in different types of sectors or territories (Becheikh, Landry, and Amara 2006) by evaluating businesses that belong to specific industrial sectors according to the Pavitt taxonomy (Pavitt 1984). We believe that our empirical validation opens the door to investigating the informal economy. To contribute to this line of research, it is necessary to investigate the causal relationships and the interconnection between competition by informal firms and the innovation behavior of formal firms at different levels, including the industry, firm, and institutional levels.

Our empirical study demonstrates that possessing the advantage of global supply chain collaboration lowers formal firms' incentive to innovate. Given the inconsistent conclusions in previous studies (Mccann and Bahl 2016; Mendi and Costamagna 2017), more research is called for to validate or refute such relationships. It is possible that to meet the demands of global partners and maintain such competitive advantages, formal firms may need to step up innovation, instead of reducing innovation. This could be a very fruitful area to study.

While our study focuses on the effect of the competition by informal firms on formal firms' innovation, and how global value chain collaboration moderates this relationship; we have not studied the direct relationship between the incentive to globalize business in formal firms and the competition by informal firms, which could be a goldmine for IB scholars. Finally, it would be worthy to investigate the question about what other strategies formal firms develop to cope with competition by informal firms. Do they expand into overseas markets or develop a closer relationship with the government to gain more support locally? Further studies are needed to address these issues (McGahan 2012; Ketchen, Duane Ireland, and Webb 2014; Darbi and Knott 2016; Mccann and Bahl 2016; Mendi and Costamagna 2017).

APPLICATIONS

Our empirical analysis demonstrates that informal competition has a positive effect on the innovation of formal firms. However, such relationship may not be a linear one and may be mitigated by the increasing use of global supply chain collaboration by Chinese formal firms. This finding has significant practical implications. Formal firms need to develop supply chain collaboration as a response strategy to sustain their competitive advantages. More specifically, first, managers in formal firms must develop their organizational core competencies to compete in an environment where there is strong competition by informal firms. Second, our investigation shows that keeping a certain level of competition by informal firms may stimulate more innovation among formal firms.

However, according to Xie, Qi, and Xiaoguo (2018), China's formal firms engage in corruption activities when faced with informal firms launching their innovation to the market, with the goal to reduce the time to obtain permits and contracts and reduce the risks of losing their innovation investment. At the same time, informal firms need to "convince" government officials to continue operations as informal firms and enjoy the advantage of lower costs (avoid paying taxes) and speed (saving time by undercutting permits). Therefore, policymakers have to strike a balance between maintaining a healthy competitive environment and cracking down on bribery and corruption from both formal and informal firms. The government should also consider developing a pathway for informal firms to become legitimate and an integrate part of the industry with legitimate competitive core competencies competing with traditional formal firms in a healthy way.

Notes

1. For more details, see the following link: http://www.enterprisesurveys.org/data/explore topics/informality.
2. Shan-Zhai refers to counterfeit or pirated fake consumer goods, including imitation and trademark infringing brands in China.
3. For more details, see the following link: http://www.enterprisesurveys.org/lac-notes

ACKNOWLEDGMENTS

We wish to thank the Guest Editors, Dr. Maoliang Bu and Dr. Tian Wei, and the anonymous reviewers for their constructive feedback, suggestions, and guidance, which helped us to lift the quality of the article.

FUNDING

This study is supported by grants from National Natural Science Foundation of China (No. 71602180; No. 71672139).

REFERENCES

Ahlstrom, D., and Z. Ding. 2014. "Enterpreneurship in China: An Overview." *International Small Business Journal: Researching Entrepreneurship* 32 (6):610–8. doi: 10.1177/0266242613517913.

Allred, B. B., and W. G. Park. 2007. "The Influence of Patent Protection on Firm Innovation Investment in Manufacturing Industries." *Journal of International Management* 13 (2):91–109. doi: 10.1016/j.intman.2007.02.001.

Barney, J. B. 1996. "The Resource-Based Theory of the Firm." *Organization Science* 7 (5):469. doi: 10.1287/orsc.7.5.469.

Barney, J. B. 2001. "Resource-Based Theories of Competitive Advantage: A Ten-Year Retrospective on the Resource-Based View." *Journal of Management* 27 (6):643–50. doi: 10.1177/014920630102700602.

Barney, J. B. 2001. "Is the Resorce-Based "View" a Useful Perspective for Strategic Management Research? Yes." *Academy of Management Review* 26 (1):41–56. doi: 10.2307/259393.

Becheikh, N., R. Landry, and N. Amara. 2006. "Lessons from Innovation Empirical Studies in the Manufacturing Sector: A Systematic Review of the Literature from 1993–2003." *Technovation* 26 (5–6):644–64. doi: 10.1016/j.technovation.2005.06.016.

Byrne, B. M. 2010. *Structural Equation Modeling with AMOS: Basic Concepts, Applications, and Programming.* 2nd ed. New York: Routledge.

Cao, M., and Q. Zhang. 2011. "Supply Chain Collaboration: Impact on Collaborative Advantage and Firm Performance." *Journal of Operations Management* 29 (3):163–80. doi: 10.1016/j.jom.2010.12.008.

Crespi, G., and P. Zuniga. 2012. "Innovation and Productivity: Evidence from Six Latin American Countries." *World Development* 40 (2):273–90. doi: 10.1016/j.worlddev.2011.07.010.

Cui, Y., J. Jiao, and H. Jiao. 2016. "Technological Innovation in Brazil, Russia, India, China, and South Africa (BRICS): An Organizational Ecology Perspective." *Technological Forecasting and Social Change* 107 (1):28–36. doi: 10.1016/j.techfore.2016.02.001.

Darbi, K., C. Hall, and P. Knott. 2018. "The Informal Sector : A Review and Agenda for Management Research." *International Journal of Management Reviews* 20 (2):301–24. doi: 10.1111/ijmr.12131.

Darbi, W. P. K., and P. Knott. 2016. "Strategising Practices in an Informal Economy Setting: A Case of Strategic Networking." *European Management Journal* 34 (4):400–13. doi: 10.1016/j.emj.2015.12.009.

Deephouse, D. L. 1999. "To Be Different, or to Be the Same? It's a Question (and Theory) of Strategic Balance." *Strategic Management Journal* 20 (2):147–66. doi: 10.1002/(SICI)1097-0266(199902)20:2<147::AID-SMJ11>3.0.CO;2-Q.

Desarbo, W. S., C. A. Di Benedetto, M. Song, and I. Sinha. 2005. "Revisiting the Miles and Snow Strategic Framework: Uncovering Interrelationships between Strategic Types, Capabilities, Environmental Uncertainty, and Firm Performance." *Strategic Management Journal* 26 (1):47–74.

Distinguin, I., C. Rugemintwari, and R. Tacneng. 2016. "Can Informal Firms Hurt Registered SMEs' Access to Credit?" *World Development* 84(August):18–40. doi: 10.1016/j.worlddev.2016.04.006.

Geldes, C., and C. Felzensztein. 2013. "Marketing Innovations in the Agribusiness Sector." *Academia Revista Latinoamericana de Administración* 26 (1):108–38. doi: 10.1108/ARLA-05-2013-0042.

Geldes, C., C. Felzensztein, and J. Palacios-Fenech. 2017. "Technological and Non-Technological Innovations, Performance and Propensity to Innovate across Industries: The Case of an Emerging Economy." *Industrial Marketing Management* 61(February):55–66. doi: 10.1016/j.indmarman.2016.10.010.

Gonzalez, A. S., and F. Lamanna. 2007. Who Fears Competition from Informal Firms ? Evidence from Latin America, World Bank Policy Research Working Paper No. 4316. Washington, DC.

Hoskisson, R. E., L. Eden, C. M. Lau, and M. Wright. 2000. "Strategy in Emerging Economies." *Academy of Management Journal* 43 (3):249–67. doi: 10.2307/1556394.

Hoskisson, R. E., M. Wright, I. Filatotchev, and M. W. Peng. 2013. "Emerging Multinationals from Mid-Range Economies: The Influence of Institutions and Factor Markets." *Journal of Management Studies* 50 (7):1295–321.

Huang, P. 2009. "China's Neglected Informal Economy Reality and Theory." *Modern China* 35 (4):405–38. doi: 10.1177/0097700409333158.

Huang, P. 2017. "China's Informal Economy, Reconsidered: An Introduction in Light of Social-Economic and Legal History." *Rural China: An International Journal of History and Social Science* 14 (1):1–17.

Iriyama, A., R. Kishore, and D. Talukdar. 2016. "Playing Dirty or Building Capability? Corruption and HR Training as Competitive Actions to Threats from Informal and Foreign Firm Rivals." *Strategic Management Journal* 37 (10):2152–73. doi: 10.1002/smj.2447.

Ketchen, David J., R. Duane Ireland, and Justin W. Webb. 2014. "Toward a Research Agenda for the Informal Economy: A Survey of the Strategic Entrepreneurship Journal's Editorial Board." *Strategic Entrepreneurship Journal* 8 (1):95–100. doi: 10.1002/sej.1175.

Khan, Z., R. Rao-Nicholson, and S. Tarba. 2018. "Global Networks as a Mode of Balance for Exploratory Innovations in a Late Liberalizing Economy." *Journal of World Business.* 53 (3):392–402. doi: 10.1016/j.jwb.2016.10.002.

Kunc, M. H., and J. D. Morecroft. 2009. "Resource-Based Strategies and Problem Structuring: Using Resource Maps to Manage Resource Systems." *Journal of the Operational Research Society* 60 (2):191–9. doi: 10.1057/palgrave.jors.2602551.

Kunc, M., and J. Morecroft. 2010. "Managerial Decision Making and Firm Performance under a Resource-Based Paradigm." *Strategic Management Journal* 31 (11):1164–82. doi: 10.1002/smj.858.

Lee, C. K., and S. Hung. 2014. "Institutional Entrepreneurship in the Informal Economy: China's Shan-Zhai Mobile Phones." *Strategic Entrepreneurship Journal* 8 (1):16–36.

Li, and K. Atuahene-Gima. 2001. "Product Innovation Strategy and the Performance of New Technology Ventures in China." *The Academy of Management Journal* 44 (6):1123–34.

Liu, H. 2017. *Chinese Business: Landscapes and Strategies*. 2nd ed. London: Routledge.

Mccann, B., and M. Bahl. 2016. "The Influence of Competition from Informal Firms on New Product Development." *Strategic Management Journal* 38 (7):1518–35. doi: 10.1002/smj.2585.

McGahan, A. 2012. "Challenges of the Informal Economy for the Field of Management." *Academy of Management Perspectives* 26 (3):12–21. doi: 10.5465/amp.2012.0104.

Mendi, P., and R. Costamagna. 2017. "Managing Innovation under Competitive Pressure from Informal Producers." *Technological Forecasting and Social Change 114 (January)* 114:192–202.

OECD/Eurostat. 2005. Manual de Oslo: Guía para la Recogida e Interpretación de Datos sobre Innovación. OCDE.

Parnell, J. 2011. "Strategic Capabilities, Competitive Strategy, and Performance among Retailers in Argentina, Peru and the United States." *Management Decision* 49 (1):139–55. doi: 10.1108/00251741111094482.

Pavitt, K. 1984. "Sectoral Patterns of Technical Change: Towards a Taxonomy and a Theory." *Research Policy* 13 (6):343–73. doi: 10.1016/0048-7333(84)90018-0.

Peng, M. 2013. "An Institution-Based View of IPR Protection." *Business Horizons* 56 (2):135–9. doi: 10.1016/j.bushor.2012.10.002.

Ramanathan, U., and A. Gunasekaran. 2014. "Supply Chain Collaboration: Impact of Success in Long-Term Partnerships." *International Journal of Production Economics* 147 (part B, January):252–9. doi: 10.1016/j.ijpe.2012.06.002.

Reed, R., and R. DeFillippi. 1990. "Causal Ambiguity, Barriers to Imitation, and Sustainable Competitive Advantage." *Academy of Management Review* 15 (1):88–102. doi: 10.5465/amr.1990.4308277.

Ren, R.,. L. Yu, and Y. Zhu. 2016. "Innovation-Orientation, Dynamic Capabilities and Evolution of the Informal Shanzhai Firms in China." *Journal of Entrepreneurship in Emerging Economies* 8 (1):45–59. doi: 10.1108/JEEE-01-2015-0003.

Ren, R., and Z. Yu. 2016. "Innovation-Orientation, Dynamic Capabilities and Evolution of the Informal Shanzhai Firms in China: A Case Study." *Journal of Entrepreneurship in Emerging Economies* 8 (1):1–12.

Royston, P. 2004. "Multiple Imputation of Missing Values." *The Stata Journal: Promoting Communications on Statistics and Stata* 4 (3):227–41. doi: 10.1177/1536867X0400400301.

Schneider, F. 2002. Size and Measurement of the informal Economy in 110 countries Around the World (Paper presented at a Workshop of Australian National Tax Centre). Canberra, Australia.

Shan, J., S. Yang, S. Yang, and J. Zhang. 2014. "An Empirical Study of the Bullwhip Effect in China." *Production and Operations Management* 23 (4):537–51. doi: 10.1111/poms.12034.

Shen, L. 2016. "China Is the Biggest Venture Capital Firm in the World." *Fortune* March 9. http://fortune.com/2016/03/09/investors-venture-capital-china/.

Soosay, C., P. Hyland, and M. Ferrer. 2008. "Supply Chain Collaboration: Capabilities for Continuous Innovation." *Supply Chain Management: An International Journal* 13 (2):160–9. doi: 10.1108/13598540810860994.

Wang, J., F. Cooke, and Z. Lin. 2016. "Informal Employment in China: Recent Development and Human Resource Implications." *Asia Pacific Journal of Human Resources* 54 (3):292–311. doi: 10.1111/1744-7941.12099.

Wang, L., D. Ahlstrom, A. Nair, and R. Hang. 2008. "Creating Globally Competitive and Innovative Products: China's Next Olympic Challenge." *SAM Advanced Management Journal* 73 (3):4–16.

Webb, J., G. Bruton, L. Tihanyi, and D. Ireland. 2013. "Research on Entrepreneurship in the Informal Economy: Framing a Research Agenda." *Journal of Business Venturing* 28 (5):598–614. doi: 10.1016/j.jbusvent.2012.05.003.

Williams, C., and A. Martinez-Perez. 2014. "Why do Consumers Purchase Goods and Services in the Informal Economy?" *Journal of Business Research* 67 (5):802–6. doi: 10.1016/j.jbusres.2013.11.048.

Williamson, P., and M. Zeng. 2009. Chinese Multinationals: Emerging through New Global Gateways. In *Emerging Multinationals in Emerging Markets*, edited by R. Ramamurti and J. V. Singh, 81–109. Cambridge: Cambridge University Press.

Xie, X., G. Qi, and K. Xiaoguo. 2018. "Corruption and New Product Innovation: Examining Firms' Ethical Dilemmas in Transition Economies." *Journal of Business Ethics* :1–19. https://doi.org/10.1007/s10551-018-3804-7.

Yang, X., and S. Terjesen. 2007. "In Search of Confidence: Context, Collaboration, and Constraints." *Asia Pacific Journal of Management* 24 (4):497–507. doi: 10.1007/s10490-007-9044-5.

Zawawi, N., S. Wahab, and A. Mamun. 2017. "Logistics Capability, Logistics Performance, and the Moderating Effect of Firm Size: Empirical Evidence from East Coast Malaysia." *The Journal of Developing Areas* 51 (2): 171–83. doi: 10.1353/jda.2017.0038.

Zhang, M., S. Sarker, and S. Sarker. 2008. "Unpacking the Effect of IT Capability on the Performance of Export-Focused SMEs: A Report from China." *Information Systems Journal* 18 (4):357–80. doi: 10.1111/j.1365-2575.2008.00303.x.

Applying Complexity Theory To Understand Chinese Consumers' Decision-Making In Innovative Products

Zhe Zhang, Yuansi Hou and Yongmin Zhu

Abstract: This study is the first to apply complexity theory to identify antecedent paths, involving perceived risks (functional risk and emotional risk), innate consumer innovativeness, and consumers' demographics related to information search (ongoing search and pre-purchase search), in the innovative products context. This study contributes a new perspective to Chinese innovation literature, using a configurational analysis, namely, fuzzy-set qualitative comparative analysis (fsQCA), which is based on an asymmetrical mode of thinking about the relationships among variables. The findings demonstrate the tenets (equifinality, complexity, and asymmetry) of configurational analysis and reveal configurations of antecedents that are sufficient for consistently predicting the conditions when perceived risk associates with information search in the innovative products context. Namely, perceived risk (functional risk and emotional risk) in recipes with innate consumer innovativeness and/or demographic antecedents are sufficient in predicting a high or low level of ongoing and pre purchase information search. This research contributes to the literature on perceived risk, information search, and innovation management, particularly in the context of Chinese innovation.

Innovation is an essential component of economic development and organizational transformation, garnering substantial focus among researchers and industries (Barczak 2012; Kotler and Keller 2012), particularly when we examine innovation in China, a country considered a potential global innovation leader (Roth, Seong, and Woetzel 2015; Woetzel et al. 2015). It has been acknowledged that innovation involves not only introducing the new products but producing a great shift in our behaviors surrounding the new products (e.g., Norden, Buston, and Wagner 2014; Zuckerman 2013), thereby driving a growing number of companies to

produce innovative products based on customers' perceived values and deepening the cus-
tomer-oriented management philosophy. Conversely, due to the complex nature of innovating
products and consumer behaviors in this age, the manner in which consumers make decisions
in adopting innovative products is complex and could constantly change—specifically, the
factor of uncertain perception of what innovative products would bring to customers in their
decision-making experience. How to control the perceived risk that is generated when customers purchase innovative products has become one of the essential topics in academia and
industry. Since innovative products differ somewhat from established products in terms of
function, appearance, and benefits, consumers typically engage far more in information
search activities to understand how such products could be used and their potential benefits.
This perceived risk is central to consumers' purchase decisions about innovative products.
Therefore, research regarding the effect of perceived risk on information search is critically
important to understanding purchasing behavior in the context of innovative products.
Consumers usually utilize information search to reduce the perceived risk; therefore,
researching on the interaction effect of perceived risk and information search carries considerable weight for controlling perceived risk and understanding innovative products adoption
behavior among Chinese consumers.

Information search is a process by which consumers make inquiries in the social environment and access appropriate data in order to make reasonable decisions (Solomon 2012).
Information search is a persistent process behavior based on a collection of selection sets
(Dellaert and Häubl 2012; Levav, Reinholtz, and Lin 2012; Pham and Chang 2010) and is
driven not only by the consumers' desire to purchase a particular product but also by their
own interests and habits before the purchase demand is generated (Bloch, Sherrell, and
Ridgway 1986). Therefore, two distinct types of information search occur: pre-purchase
search and ongoing search (Bloch, Sherrell, and Ridgway 1986; Dholakia 1998, 2001). Pre-
purchase search refers to a consumer's search for specific information in response to purchase demands, while the ongoing search refers to the consumer's broader information-seeking behaviors targeted maintaining and upgrading personal knowledge. Most prior research
on information search was conducted in the non-innovative product context and, thus,
focuses on pre-purchase search (Bloch, Sherrell, and Ridgway 1986). However, advances in
information technology and the Internet enable companies to stimulate market interest before
products are officially launched. The time interval between prerelease and official launch for
new products continues to increase (Iyer and Davenport 2008).

This new marketing strategy, which has become highly popular for innovative products,
creates more opportunities for consumers to engage in ongoing search activities. Huawei, one
of the leading Chinese innovative companies, is an example. The Huawei Watch was prereleased in Mobile World Congress on March 1, 2015 but was not listed for sale for nearly
half a year later, on September 2, 2015 (Huawei.com 2015). Therefore, the impact of
ongoing search is considered a potentially crucial factor in the marketing of innovative products.

In addition, an individual trait called innate consumer innovativeness plays an important
role in understanding the adoption of innovative products (Hirunyawipada and Paswan 2006;
Lee, Lee, and Garrett 2013; Vandecasteele and Geuens 2010). Individuals have different

preferences for and tendencies to make innovative decisions or use innovative products (Hauser and Toubia 2005; Midgley and Dowling 1978). Innate consumer innovativeness refers to an inherent and unobservable characteristic that reflects an individual's tendency to innovate (Hirschman 1980; Hoffman, Kopalle, and Novak 2010). When applied in the specific domain of innovative products, innate consumer innovativeness represents a psychological trait that determines the degree to which a person will embrace newly released innovative products (Goldsmith and Hofacker 1991; Klink and Athaide 2010; Li, Zhang, and Wang 2015). Therefore, exploring whether or not the degree of innate consumer innovativeness influences the relationship between perceived risk and information search is worthwhile.

Empirical findings of the relationship between perceived risk and information search reveal inconsistencies. Some prior research shows that information search and perceived risk relate positively (e.g., Chaudhuri 1997; Murray 1991; Srinivasan and Ratchford 1991). Information search is an important factor that can affect perceived risks. It frequently reduces the risks that consumers encounter when evaluating products or services (Mitra, Reiss, and Capella 1999), and consumers readily employ it as a strategy to address perceived risk (Bloch, Sherrell, and Ridgway 1986). Although scholars suggest that perceived risk has a positive effect on information search, Gemunden (1985) finds that among more than 100 empirical studies, 51% of the research demonstrated no significant relationship or negative correlation between perceived risk and information search. Conchar et al. (2004) suggest that information search can be a consequence of perceived risk rather than a proxy for perceived risk.

Urry (2005) suggests that relationships between variables can be nonlinear with abrupt switches occurring; therefore, the same "cause" can, in specific contexts, produce different effects. The current study advances an asymmetric stance to overcome the limitations of symmetric stance. Urry's complexity turn indicates that whether the antecedent condition is positively or negatively related to an outcome condition depends on the particular complex configuration of other antecedents.

Therefore, the positioning of this study is to investigate the relationship between perceived risks (functional risk and emotional risk) and information search (ongoing search and pre-purchase search) to understand the Chinese consumers' innovative products adoption behavior. In contrast to the prior research, this study addresses the complexity in this relationship by applying a method of configurational analysis, which is called fuzzy-set qualitative comparative analysis (fsQCA), which is based on an asymmetrical mode of considering relationships among variables. The purpose is to investigate how configurations of antecedent conditions involving perceived risks (functional risk and emotional risk) relate to information search (ongoing search and pre-purchase search) in the innovative products context, providing a new and useful approach to address this complex research question among Chinese innovation product consumers.

The remainder of this article is organized as follows. The next section provides a brief review of prior research related to perceived risk and information search. The third section introduces fsQCA as a configurational approach to present the antecedent recipes associated with perceived risk, consumer innovativeness and information search. The article then illustrates the empirical study method to test the theory. The next section analyzes the data

and provides the findings, and the last section presents a discussion of the results, contribution to theory and practice, study's limitations, and suggestions for future research.

PERCEIVED RISK AND INFORMATION SEARCH IN THE INNOVATIVE PRODUCTS CONTEXT

Many scholars have conducted research on the dimensions of perceived risk (e.g., Kaplan,
Szybillo, and Jacoby 1974; Roselius 1971), which suggests that perceived risk is a multidi-
mensional concept. Roselius (1971) believes that consumers bear the risk of loss when making purchasing decisions; this includes time loss, hazard loss, ego loss, and money loss.
Kaplan, Szybillo, and Jacoby (1974) use regression analysis to determine the relationship
between five components (physical risk, psychological risk, social risk, financial risk, and
performance risk) of risks and overall perceived risk across 12 products. The study finds that
these five components can explain 74 percent of the variance of the overall risk. Thereafter,
Murray and Schlacter (1990) conduct further research on the concept of perceived risk.
Financial risk is associated with money and risk capital; physical risk refers to physical,
health, and energy aspects of loss; performance risk arises when products deliver functions
and meet the needs of customers; social risk relates to the possible loss of respect and friend-
ship with others when purchasing or using the products; psychosocial risk refers to the potential damage to self-image in the process of the product purchase or product. Chaudhuri
(2000) conducted principal component analysis on these five aspects of perceived risk and
extracted two factors, namely, functional risk and emotional risk. Specifically, functional risk
relates to financial, performance, and physical risks, and emotional risk reflects the social
and psychological risks. This study adopts the concepts of the two dimensions of perceived
risk—functional risk and emotional risk—to analyze the impact of the perceived risk on the
information search of innovative products.

Information search not only includes pre-purchase information search that is related to
specific product demands but also ongoing information search that is driven by consumers'
personal interests and habits before purchase demand is generated (Bloch, Sherrell, and
Ridgway 1986). However, in prior studies, most researchers consider only pre-purchase
search. Consumers conduct pre-purchase information search to increase product knowledge
that enables them to make better purchasing decisions, which results in higher satisfaction
with those decisions. Conversely, by continuously engaging in ongoing information search,
consumers gain general product knowledge.

Innovative products differ from ordinary products in terms of functionality or appearance,
which makes questions difficult for consumers to answer regarding whether or not they are
useful and how to use them (Chakravarti and Xie 2006). Hence, innovative products are associated with higher perceived risk. When consumers believe the risk associated with purchasing innovative products is high, their purchase intentions decrease (Cox 1967; Stone and
Gronhaug 1993).

Booz Allen Hamilton (1982) classify the innovative products and services into six
categories based on two dimensions, newness to the company and newness to the market.

The categories are as follows: new-to-the-world products, new product lines, additions to existing product lines, improvements to existing products, re-positioning, and cost reductions. The innovative products and services proffered by Product Development and Management Association (PDMA) include two types (PDMA 2017). The first one is radical innovation, which refers to the really-new products that generally involve new technology and are able to significantly change consumer behavior and consumption paradigm in the market. Radical innovation corresponds to the first type of innovative product raised by Booz Allen Hamilton (1982), new-to-the-world products. The other is incremental innovation products that improve the conveyance of a currently delivered benefit not produce the behavior or consumption change. Incremental innovation products cover the remaining five categories of innovative products and services suggested by Booz and Hamilton (1982) (e.g. new product lines, additions to existing product lines, improvements to existing products, re-positioning, and cost reductions). This study adopts the definition and categorization by PDMA and focuses on the incremental innovation products to conduct further analysis.

Synthesizing the results of previous studies, we divide perceived risk into functional risk and emotional risk (Chaudhuri 2000), and information search into pre-purchase search and ongoing search (Bloch et al. 1986). We then explore the various effects of different dimensions of perceived risk on information search behavior.

THEORETICAL CONFIGURATIONS OF THE EFFECT OF PERCEIVED RISK ON INFORMATION SEARCH

Configurational Model

In reality, very often most contexts include asymmetrical relationships and rarely include symmetrical ones (Ragin 2008). Greckhamer (2011) utilizes the configurational approach to investigate the combinations of cultural and macro-environmental attributes, which are associated with the differences existing in the compensation level and the compensation inequality. Hsiao et al. (2015) offer asymmetric empirical models via qualitative comparative analysis for all four sets of relationships of happy/unhappy and highly unproductive/ productive employees. The researchers find that cases exist in nearly all large data sets that run counter to the main effects relationship. The limitations of using symmetric statistical tests to empirically examine theoretical relationships have led researchers to call for building and testing theory using algorithms from an asymmetric stance (Grandori and Furnari 2008).

Ragin (2006) proffers theory and provides fsQCA to build a model and test empirical relationships that consistently identify cases with high (or low) focal outcomes. The idea of fsQCA is to investigate how a conjunctive statement of antecedent conditions ("causal recipes"; Ragin 2008), rather than individual antecedents, lead to an un/favorable conclusion or decision (Feurer, Baumbach, and Woodside 2016; Hsiao et al. 2015). Mathematically, fsQCA has no sample size limits (see also Fiss 2011; Ragin and Fiss 2009), which makes fsQCA a powerful tool for a wide array of research problems in management. fsQCA bridges quantitative and qualitative methods in that "fuzzy sets have many of the virtues of conventional interval- and ratio-scale variables, but at the same time they permit qualitative assessment" (Ragin 2008).

Several tenets are probed in the study of antecedent conditions affecting an outcome by configurational analysis. The first tenet of configurational analysis is "equifinality," that is, "a few (not one) of the many possible paths lead to the same outcome" (Wu et al. 2014). Equifinality assumes that two or more configurations can be equally effective in increasing searching behaviors within the same context (Hsiao et al. 2015). Thus, no one combination is necessary for accurately predicting customers' information search.

The second tenet of complexity is that relationships between variables can be nonlinear with abrupt switches occurring, and therefore, the same "cause" can, in specific circumstances, produce different effects (Urry 2005). The complexity tenet supports a shift from reductionist analyses to the study of complex vital matter that remains on "the edge of chaos" (Urry 2005). Hence, the configurational analysis focus transfers from examining the net effect or total effects to the study of alternative causal configurations, which consistently lead to a given outcome of interest (cf. Ragin 1997), such as customers' perceived risk or information search.

The tenet of causal asymmetry is also stressed by configurational analysis. The causal asymmetry tenet indicates that the causes (recipes) leading to the rejection of an outcome are unique and not the mirror opposites of causes (recipes) of acceptance of the outcome (Ragin 2008; Woodside 2014). This tenet suggests that no one factor is sufficient, or likely necessary, for an outcome, and that research focusing only on the presence of an outcome of interest is unlikely to be very informative regarding the causes of the absence of the outcome (Ragin 2008; Woodside 2014). The tenet of causal asymmetry indicates that high perceived risk appears in algorithms associated with more information search; it does not mean that low perceived risk is a necessary ingredient in all configurations that lead to less information search. Furthermore, other tenets may suggest that "unique complex antecedent configurations are sufficient but not necessary for high scores in an outcome condition" and that "simple antecedent conditions can be necessary. However, they are insufficient for indicating high scores in an outcome condition" (Wu et al. 2014).

In this research, Venn diagrams (Dușa 2007) are used to model the causal configuration of complex antecedent conditions leading to perceived risk (functional risk and emotional risk) and information search (ongoing search and pre-purchase search) (see Figure 1). The arrows in the Venn diagrams illustrate testable propositions of principal associations: (1) the influence of demographic configurations on configurations of perceived risk (functional risk and emotional risk); (2) the influence of configurations of perceived risk (functional risk and emotional risk) on ongoing product information search; (3) the influence of configurations of perceived risk (functional risk and emotional risk) on pre-purchase search; and (4) innate consumer innovativeness plays a moderating role in the effects of perceived risk on information search (ongoing search and pre-purchase search). The methodological approach elucidates the causal relationship between the characteristics of a configuration and an outcome of interest.

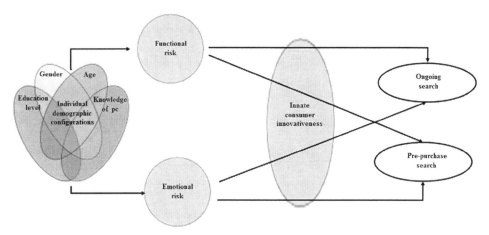

FIGURE 1. Configurational Model

Relevancy of Demographics to Perceived Risk

The literature on the net effects of consumer demographic variables on perceived risk is large, which suggests that the levels of perceived risk vary with the person (Hoover, Green, and Saegert 1978; Peter and Ryan 1976). Garbarino and Strahilevitz (2004) study how males and females differ in their perception of online shopping risks. Since perceived online purchase risk decreases as Internet usage increases (Kehoe, Pitkow, and Morton 1998; Miyazaki and Fernandez 2001), they control Internet usage and find that females perceive greater online purchasing risk than males (Garbarino and Strahilevitz 2004). Phillips and Sternthal (1977) indicate that "age differences result in a complex set of changes in individuals' sources of information, ability to learn, and susceptibility to social influence," which can lead to different levels of perceived risk. Mitchell (2001) also suggests that the elderly have more effective means to decrease risks.

In addition to gender and age, education can also affect perceived risk. Spence, Engel, and Blackwell (1970) find a slightly inverse relationship between the level of perceived risk and the number of years of education. This finding is true when a product is bought from a store. However, when the same product is purchased by mail, the researchers do not find the same relationship. In addition, evidence shows that customers who belong to "lower education and larger family demographic clusters may purchase more extended warranties to reduce financial and performance risk" (Center for Policy Alternatives 1978).

Configurations of the Effect of Perceived Risk On Ongoing Search

Consumers adopt different decision modes based on context. A consumer's cognitive style and decision-making mode change with the decision-making environment. Therefore, different dimensions of perceived risk have different effects on information search behaviors (Mitchell 1999).

Many scholars have suggested that information search and perceived risk are positively related (e.g., Chaudhuri 1997; Murray 1991; Srinivasan and Ratchford 1991). However, certain studies (e.g., Gemunden 1985) have found a negative relationship or no relationship between perceived risk and information search. Thus, a high level of perceived risk alone is neither sufficient nor necessary for a high level of information search.

Ongoing information search is not related to specific purchases. Instead, consumers engage in ongoing search when they do not have specific purchase demands. The purpose of ongoing search is not to make better immediate purchasing decisions, but to make future purchasing decisions more enjoyable, to satisfy personal interests and gain product knowledge. In other words, ongoing search is related to entertainment or recreation in the present, and generates product knowledge that can be used by the consumers or others in future decision-making situations.

Will customers make an increased or reduced information search when the functional risks of innovative products create excessive anxiety? Before consumers engage in ongoing information search related to recently launch innovative products, they possess minimal functional information (e.g., price, application). By engaging in ongoing information search, consumers access not only detailed product information but also opinions about product features, price, and safety issues. Thus, accessing more information may actually have the effect of increasing consumers' perceived risk rather than reducing it. Mitchell (1999) believes that consumers deliberately avoid information that may cause cognitive dissonance, and this avoidance behavior is more likely to occur in ongoing information search, which is not related to immediate decision-making. Because consumers engage in ongoing information search for pleasure or to satisfy personal curiosity, such information search behavior is not obligatory. Since innovative products differ from other general merchandise in function or appearance, it may be difficult for consumers to discern how to use them and whether they are helpful.

However, emotional risk may have a different effect on ongoing information search than functional risk. When innovative products are prereleased, detailed information, such as features and price, are not disclosed to the public. Therefore, when searching for information, consumers tend to perceive the risks of innovative products from an emotional perspective (e.g., how others would evaluate them if they used the product and whether using the product would create other problems.). Emotional risk is the main problem that consumers want to mitigate when they engage in ongoing search; thus, emotional risk affects ongoing search behavior.

Innate consumer innovativeness is an essential factor that affects consumer decision-making regarding innovative products (Im, Bayus, and Mason 2003). As Cowart, Fox, and Wilson's (2008) study on consumer innovativeness and self-consistency shows, consumer innovativeness and perceived risk have a positive relationship with behavioral intention. For instance, highly innovative consumers have low levels of perceived risk and high levels of purchasing willingness. Bloch, Sherrell, and Ridgway (1986) report that individuals who engage more in ongoing information search are more likely to be opinion leaders; similarly, opinion leaders tend to be more innovative. According to Kirton's (1976) definition of innovativeness, highly innovative individuals prefer variation and are more inclined to accept new things. Conversely, innovative consumers prefer adventures and are more open to new experiences; therefore, their self-concepts adjust more easily to change. Ongoing information search enables people to access more new information, which is consistent with innovative consumers' demands for novelty. Hence, the level of innovativeness may modify the relationship between perceived risk and ongoing information search. Therefore we propose as follows:

> *Hypothesis 1: Perceived risk (functional risk and emotional risk) in recipes with innate consumer innovativeness and/or demographic antecedents are sufficient in predicting a high or low level of ongoing information search.*

Configurations of the Effect of Perceived Risk on Pre-Purchase Search

Pre-purchase search is based on improving satisfaction with a specific purchase as well as obtaining information. That is, when consumers have previously considered purchasing a product, pre-purchase information search improves satisfaction by reducing perceived risk. The accumulated information obtained through ongoing search can make future pre-purchase information search and purchase behavior more efficient (Bettman 1979).

Consumers frequently use information search to reduce perceived functional risks such as financial risk, performance risk, and physical risk. In contrast to established products, the product knowledge accumulated through ongoing information search for innovative products is very limited. In addition, prior research has shown that individuals who are knowledgeable or unknowledgable engage less in information search than somewhat-knowledgeable individuals (Bettman and Park 1980). Therefore, in the context of pre-purchase information search, consumers who perceive a comparatively high level of functional risk may not engage more in information search activities than consumers who perceive a comparatively low level of functional risk. In fact, it is possible that such individuals may engage less in information search activities to avoid cognitive dissonance.

However, consumers reduce emotional risk by soliciting the opinions of others, which is generally unrelated to knowledge level. Consumers who engage in pre-purchase information search activities have previously decided to purchase (and, therefore, to accept social and psychological risks associated with) innovative products. Since social risk is external as opposed to internal risk, although consumers are able to avoid information that conflicts with their self-concept, they cannot change others' evaluations of themselves once they use the product. Therefore, consumers may seek more information and opinions about an innovative product to minimize the conflict between the product and their self-concept.

Innate consumer innovativeness also modifies the effects of perceived risk on pre-purchase information search. Brucks (1985) suggested that consumers who make innovative decisions need relatively minimal information. Since highly innovative consumers are more likely to accept new things, and are more receptive to innovative products, they require less information than others to make satisfactory decisions about innovative products. Therefore,

TABLE 1.
Sample Profile

Demographic variables	Summary
Gender	Male: 61.9%
	Female: 38.1%
Age	Minimum = 14
	Maximum = 74
	Mean = 28.6
Highest education level	1 (High School or Below); 2 (Some College); 3 (Bachelor's Degree); 4 (Masters/Some Graduate School)
	Mean = 2.67
Knowledge of Tablet PCs	1 (None); 2 (Too Little); 3 (A Little); 4 (Some); 5 (Quite a Bit); 6 (An Extreme Amount)
	Mean = 4.04

consumer innovativeness influences the relationship between perceived risk and pre-purchase search. Accordingly, we hypothesize as follows:

Hypothesis 2: Perceived risk (functional risk and emotional risk), in recipes with consumer innovativeness and/or demographic antecedents, are sufficient in predicting pre-purchase search.

METHODS

Data Collection

A survey methodology was used to gather data for the research. Data collection was accomplished through a two-stage process. First, we conducted a pilot study where online questionnaires were randomly distributed to 120 university students. Based on the feedback, we revised and finalized the research stimulus and response scales. Second, we repeated the process in the main study where participants were first requested to read a paragraph with a detailed description of a recently launched version of tablet PC and answer a screening question, indicating whether they believed the version of tablet PC was an innovative product. Then, respondents answered survey questions related to perceived risk, pre-purchase information search, ongoing information search, consumer innovativeness, and demographic information.

In total, 360 participants took the survey, and there were 239 valid responses (including complete demographics), yielding a response rate of 66.4%. Responses from participants who did not pass the screening test (i.e., those who believed the tablet PC was not an innovative product) were eliminated from further analysis. The final data set included responses from 134 participants. The sample profile is shown in Table 1.

To examine whether the sample had a self-selection bias, we compared the demographic information of the two groups: the final data set with 134 valid responses, and the excluded data set with 105 responses. No significant differences were found. Finally, according to the statistics provided by an online community manager, the highly educated participants in this study adequately represented early adopters of innovative products. Therefore, the sample we used in this research is representative for studying innovative products (Table 1).

Stimulus

A recently launched version of a tablet PC was selected as the research stimulus to represent an innovative product. A tablet PC is a personal computer that is small in size but full-featured. A tablet's appearance is similar to a laptop, but it is superior in terms of mobility and portability. The concept of a tablet PC was first proposed by Microsoft®, and on January 28, 2010, Apple® released its own version, the iPad.® Currently, many consumers are choosing tablet PCs as their second laptops. We used an innovative version of the tablet PC as our research stimulus for several reasons. First, an innovative version of tablet PC is a different and newer type of laptop, which is in accordance with our definition of an innovative product. Second, as a specific type of laptop, a tablet PC requires a high level of consumer involvement. Consumers are highly engaged in information search when products are complex to operate and the products require high levels of personal involvement. Third, both types of perceived risk are represented in the innovative version of tablet PC purchasing behavior.

Measures

We measured consumers' perceived risks associated with innovative products and the levels of ongoing and pre-purchase information search driven by the perceived risks. Furthermore, innate consumer innovativeness was also measured to assess its moderating effect. Based on knowledge obtained through in-depth interviews and our literature review, we modified existing scales to the innovative products context. We used 5-point Likert-type scales in this study, ranging from 1 (strongly disagree) to 5 (strongly agree).

Outcome measures

Consumers' ongoing information search behavior. We adapted five items used by Bloch, Sherrell, and Ridgway (1986) (e.g., "I often visit computer malls, just to look around or get information, rather than to make a specific purchase") to measure ongoing information search behavior. We combined the five survey questions into a scale that showed very good reliability ($\alpha = 0.89$). Based on the scale, we created a fuzzy set measures of membership in the set of consumers with high ongoing search, coding membership as fully out for a response of "strongly disagree" and fully in for a response of "strongly agree." The crossover point was the median of the scale (=3.40, i.e., approximately the 50th percentile).

Consumers' Pre-purchase Information Search Behavior. We adapted thirteen items used by Claxton, Fry, and Portis (1974) (e.g., "Before purchasing, I will consider alternate

TABLE 2.
Factor Analysis for Perceived Risks

	Factor 1	Factor 2
Functional risk		
Financial risk	0.73	
Performance risk	0.80	
Physical risk	0.70	
Emotional risk		
Social risk		0.73
Psychological risk		0.67

Notes: Table 2 shows the rotated factor loading matrix. The numbers in table shows the correlation of the five dimensions of perceived risks to the extracted factors (functional risk and emotional risk).

brands") to measure pre-purchase information search behavior. The items were, again, aggregated into a scale that showed acceptable reliability with a Cronbach's coefficient alpha of 0.76, which is above the preferable value of 0.70 (DeVellis 2003). Using this scale, we created a fuzzy set measures of membership in the set of consumers with high pre-purchase search, coding membership as "fully out" for a response of "strongly disagree" and "fully in" for a response of "strongly agree". The crossover point was the median of the scale (=3.92, i.e., approximately the 50th percentile).

Independent measures Perceived Risk. To measure perceived risk, we based our survey fifteen items on those used by Stone and Gronhaug (1993) (e.g., "If I bought this product, I feel that it would be a bad way to spend my money"). In accordance with the method used by Chaudhuri (2000), the study included using principal component analysis to analyze five dimensions of perceived risk. Two factors, functional risk and emotional risk, were extracted with a total explained variance of 70.5 percent. The rotated component matrix appears in Table 2. In subsequent analyses, we used the factor scores to represent functional risk and emotional risk. The items were aggregated into two scales that showed strong reliability (functional risk: $\alpha = 0.85$; emotional risk: $\alpha = 0.79$)

Using these scales, we created two fuzzy set measures. Membership in the set of consumers with functional risk was coded as fully out for a minimum observed value of scale (=1) and fully in for a maximum observed value of scale (=4.73). For a crossover point, we chose the product of the 50th percentile values of scale (=2.73). Coding of membership in the set of consumers with emotional risk acted in accordance with the same approach. Membership in the set of consumers with emotional risk was coded as "fully out" for a minimum value of scale (=1) and "fully in" for a maximum value of scale (=4.63). For a crossover point, we chose the product of the 50th percentile values of scale (=2.63).

Innate Consumer Innovativeness. We adapted the Domain-Specific Innovativeness (DSI) Scale developed by Goldsmith and Hofacker (1991) to measure consumer innovativeness (e.g., "In general, I am the first in my circle of friends to know the functions of the latest tablet PC"). The seven items that consist in the original scale were combined into a scale that showed very good reliability ($\alpha = 0.85$).The fuzzy set measure of innate consumer innovativeness was based on this scale and coded as "fully out" of the set for value 1 ("strongly disagree"). Because the maximum observed value was 5 ("strongly agree"), we coded this value as "fully in" the set of innate consumer innovativeness. We used the 50th percentile values of 3.14 as the crossover point.

Gender. Male was coded as full membership in the context of innovative digital product and female was coded as full non-membership.

Age. Age ranging from 18 to 45 was coded as full membership; others were full non-membership.

Education Level. Answers to this question were measured on four levels (high school or below, some college, bachelor's degree, and masters/some graduate school). We coded consumers with a degree at the high school or below level as fully out of the set of consumers with a high education level, and consumers with a degree at the bachelor or above level as fully in the set, using "some college" level as the crossover point.

Knowledge of Tablet PCs. The answer to this question was measured on a six-point scale. Using this scale, we created a fuzzy set measure. Membership in the set of consumers with knowledge of tablet PCs was coded as fully out for a value of 1 ("none") and fully in for a value of 6 ("an extreme amount"); the scale midpoint of 3.5 was the crossover point.

Calibration

To use Boolean algebra to create complex configurations, we calibrated all variables into fuzzy-set scores range from 0 to 1, which specify the degree of membership for each case. Calibrated scores are membership scores resulting from calibrating original or interval scores and not probabilities: "In essence, a fuzzy membership score attaches a truth value, not a probability, to a statement" (Ragin 2008). Criteria for three breakpoints are necessary to perform fuzzy-set calibration: 0.05 for the threshold for full non-membership; 0.95 for the threshold of full membership; and 0.50 for the crossover point of the maximum ambiguity score between non-membership and membership (Ragin 2008). The fsQCA program (Ragin et al. 2006) provides a logarithmic function subroutine that calibrates original scores into logarithmic membership scores. When we specify the original values for these three breakpoints, the fsQCA program calibrates other remaining scores. Thus, the fuzzy sets offer a middle path between quantitative and qualitative measurement but transcend many of the limitations of both (Ragin 2008).

Table 3 delineates the calibrated value for antecedents and outcome conditions, as well as full membership, non-membership and crossover points for them. Gender is a dichotomous condition with 1 indicating male (full membership) and 0 indicating female (full non-membership). Age is calibrated as a crisp set, with 1 indicating ages ranging from 18 to 45 (full membership), and 0 indicating other ages (full non-membership).

TABLE 3.
Fuzzy Sets Calibration

Measures	Variable	95%	50%	5%
Outcome measures	Ongoing search	5	3.40	1
	Pre-purchase search	5	3.92	1
Independent measures	Functional risk	4.73	2.73	1
	Emotional risk	4.63	2.63	1
	Innate consumer innovativeness	5	3.14	1
	Highest education level	3	2	1
	Knowledge of tablet PCs	6	3.5	1
		1		0
	Gender	Male		Female
	Age		18 ~ 45	others

ANALYSIS

Configurations for Ongoing Search

We use the notation for the presence of a condition. Circles with a cross-out ("⊗") indicate its absence. Furthermore, large circles indicate core conditions, and small circles refer to peripheral conditions. Blank spaces in a solution indicate a "don't care" situation in which the causal condition may be either present or absent. Solutions are grouped by their core conditions (Ragin and Fiss 2009).

Table 4 shows the results of our fuzzy set analysis of ongoing search. The solution table shows that the fuzzy set analysis results in one solution exhibiting acceptable consistency (0.75) (Fiss 2011) and furthermore indicates the presence of both core and peripheral conditions. Hypothesis 1 is verified.

Regarding core conditions, solutions 1a, 1b, and 1c indicate that innate consumer innovativeness and gender are sufficient for achieving a high level of ongoing search. Moreover, building on the necessary analysis condition test (Ragin 2000), a combination of innate consumer innovativeness and gender is a necessary condition.

These solutions, furthermore, suggest that, with innate consumer innovativeness and gender, there are tradeoffs among functional risk, emotional risk, highest education level, knowledge of tablet PCs, and age. Specifically, solutions 1b and 1c of Table 4 indicate that in the absence of high functional risk and emotional risk, two greater conditions among highest education level, knowledge of Tablet PCs, and age allow for a high level of ongoing search regardless of whether another condition is high or not. In contrast, solution 1a shows the opposite pattern. In the presence of the highest education level, knowledge of tablet PCs, and age, functional risk and emotional risk may be either high or low, as indicated by the blank space for functional risk and emotional risk that signal a "don't care" situation for that causal condition. Comparing solutions 1a to 1b and 1c, thus, indicates that the functional risk and emotional risk and two high conditions among highest education level, knowledge of Tablet PCs and age, can be treated as substitutes. Finally, Table 5 shows the negative effect of perceived risk on ongoing search and the positive effect on innate consumer Innovativeness and demographics on ongoing search.

TABLE 4.
Configurations for Ongoing Search

	Solution		
	1a	1b	1c
Functional risk		⊗	⊗
Emotional risk		⊗	⊗
Innate consumer innovativeness	●	●	●
Highest education level	●		
Knowledge of Tablet PCs	●	●	●
Gender	●	●	●
Age	●	●	
Consistency	0.92	0.96	0.97
Raw coverage	0.43	0.39	0.38
Unique coverage	0.09	0.05	0.04
Overall solution consistency		0.92	
Overall solution coverage		0.53	

TABLE 5.
Necessary Analysis Condition Test

	Consistency	Coverage	Z-score
Innate consumer innovativeness + Gender	0.93	0.64	3.65***
Gender	0.72	0.62	−2.42
Innate consumer innovativeness	0.82	0.86	0.47

$p < 0.05$, **$p < 0.01$, ***$p < 0.001$, one-tailed tests; benchmark: 0.8.

The table also lists coverage scores that indicate the percentage of cases that take a given path to the outcome, allowing us to evaluate the importance of different causal paths (Fiss 2007). In terms of overall coverage, the combined models represent approximately 52 percent of membership in the outcome.

In accordance with an asymmetric understanding of causality in configurations, a fuzzy set analysis of the absence of a high level of ongoing search indicates no consistently identifiable solution, and consistency scores for all solutions remained considerably below the acceptable level of 0.75 (Fiss 2007, 2011). These findings indicate the absence of a clear set-theoretic relationship when either the absence of a high level of ongoing search or the presence of a low level of ongoing search is used as the outcome.

Configurations for Pre-Purchase Search

Table 6 shows the results for a fuzzy set analysis of pre-purchase search. The results indicate the existence of four distinct configurational groupings, which, again, suggests the presence of crossed-type equifinality. Hypothesis 2 is corroborated.

TABLE 6.
Configurations for Pre-Purchase Search

	Solution			
	1	*2*	*3*	*4*
Functional risk	⊗	⊗	●	
Emotional risk		●	⊗	●
Innate consumer innovativeness				●
Highest education level	●	•	•	•
Knowledge of Tablet PCs	●		⊗	•
Gender	⊗	⊗		⊗
Age	•	•	●	•
Consistency	0.94	0.95	0.97	0.93
Raw coverage	0.23	0.21	0.36	0.19
Unique coverage	0.02	0.01	0.11	0.01
Overall solution consistency		0.92		
Overall solution coverage		0.55		

Solution 1 indicates that the existence of a successful hybrid configuration that combines high education and knowledge of Tablet PCs with a low score for females on functional risk as core conditions. Solution 2 indicates that, for female consumers, high score on emotional risk produces a positive effect on pre-purchase search, whereas high score on functional risk produces a negative effect on pre-purchase search. Solution 3 indicates that, for people who know more about Tablet PCs, functional risk produces a negative effect on pre-purchase search, whereas emotional risk produces a positive effect on pre-purchase search. Finally, Solution 4 suggests that female consumers who have highly innate innovativeness are willing to do a pre-purchase search.

In terms of coverage, the solution represents approximately 55 percent of set membership in the high level of pre-purchase search group, which is more than for the analysis of a high level of ongoing search.

Similarly to configurations for ongoing search, in accordance with an asymmetric understanding of causality in configurations, a fuzzy set analysis of the absence of a high level of pre-purchase search indicates no consistently identifiable solution, and consistency scores for all solutions remained considerably below the acceptable level of 0.75. These findings indicate the absence of a clear set-theoretical relationship when either the absence of a high level of pre-purchase search or the presence of a low level of pre-purchase search is used as the outcome.

Robustness Checks

In accordance with Fiss (2011) and Garcia-Castro and Francoeur's (2016) recommendations, we conducted robustness checks to verify that the results shown hold under different calibrations. First, we varied the threshold of consistency to 0.9. No substantive changes are observed in terms of the relations depicted in Tables 4 and 5. Furthermore, we increased the frequency cutoff to 3. Minor changes are observed, as well as the specific number of solutions and sub-solutions, but the interpretation of the results remains substantively unchanged. Finally, we varied the crossover points between +/-10 percent for all measures. Similarly to the change in the frequency cutoff, minor changes are observed; however, the interpretation of the results remains substantively unchanged.

DISCUSSION

To understand the complex Chinese consumers' behaviors in adopting innovative products, we analyzed the effect of perceived risk, innate consumer innovativeness, and consumers' demographic background on information searching behaviors in a more detailed fashion by using configurational analysis.

This study suggests that the impact of perceived risks (functional risk and emotional risk) on information search (ongoing search and pre-purchase search) depends on configurations of consumer demographics and consumer innovativeness in the innovative products context among Chinese consumers. Prior research focuses on whether or not perceived risks affect information search and whether or not the influence is always positive. Instead of narrowly focusing on perceived risks and information search, a new configurational perspective has been offered here that is essential to understanding the combinations of complex conditions, namely, when high level of information search is related to configurations of consumer demographics and innate consumer innovativeness.

In contrast to attempting to build and test models for positive or negative outcomes of information search, configuration theory and fsQCA are asymmetric in focus (Ragin 2008; Fiss 2007, 2011). Therefore, a key finding of the current study is what factors are included in the configurations leading to high level of information search by consumers in the innovative products context.

First, configurational analysis is a helpful lens because whether simple antecedent conditions relate to an outcome condition of interest positively or negatively, or not at all, depends on the complex antecedent conditions. Thus, from the perspective of configurational analysis, presence/absence of perceived risk (functional risk or emotional risk) alone is not sufficient or necessary to predict and explain a high level of information search (ongoing search or pre-purchase search). Several ingredients acting in combination result in complex configurations that are sufficient in explaining and predicting high information search.

Furthermore, the objective of our study was to find out the role that innate consumer innovativeness plays in both ongoing and pre-purchase searches. Across all configurations for ongoing search and one configuration for pre-purchase search, innate consumer innovativeness is shown to be the core condition. Although innovation research acknowledges the importance of innate consumer innovativeness, prior research seldom simultaneously examines the effect of innate consumer innovativeness in both ongoing search and pre-purchase search. The current study provides empirical evidence to strongly support the central role of innate consumer innovativeness in shaping searching behavior.

Finally, the interesting finding of our study is that it clearly shows the role played by demographics when consumers search innovative products. Configurations in Tables 4 and 6 show the opposite results of how gender influences ongoing search and pre-purchase search. Furthermore, an accordance with Dwivedi, Joshi, and Misangyi's (2018) method, we tested our idea in two different situations, including gender (male/female subgroup) and age (18 ~ 45/others subgroup). Interestingly, we found that male consumers are strongly related to on-going search, whereas female consumers would attach great importance to the pre-purchase search. Furthermore, as the major consumer group for innovative products, individuals in the age group of 18 to 45 would contribute to both ongoing search and pre-purchase search.

The findings support the tenets of configurational analysis. The multiple configurations leading to high level of information search (ongoing search and pre-purchase search) confirm the first tenet of equifinality. All configurations in the study include complex antecedent conditions, including several demographic characteristics, and indicate high value in the outcome condition for information search. For example, Table 6 indicates the existence of four distinct configurational groupings, which, again, suggests the presence of across-type equifinality. Solution 1a, 1b, and 1c in Table 4 rely on the innate consumer innovativeness and gender. The solutions also show the clear tradeoffs, with perceived risk and education level substituting for each other, and allowing for neutral permutations around the core condition, indicating the presence of within-type equifinality.

The findings support the second tenet of complexity. For example, the configurations shown in Table 6 indicate that the simple antecedent conditions are not always positive or negative or always present in different complex antecedent conditions associating with the high level scores for pre-purchase search. For different segments, there are tradeoffs between functional risk and emotional risk for effect on high level pre-purchase search. Thus, achieving high information search is a complex undertaking that is difficult to describe or understand by examining the net effect or total effects.

The findings confirm the tenet of causal asymmetry. The configurations associating high level of information search (ongoing search and pre-purchase search) are not the mirror opposites of the configurations associating with the absence of high level of information search or the presence of low level of information search. The fuzzy set analysis of the absence of high level of information search indicated no consistently identifiable solution.

Managerial Implications

Since perceived risk is an important factor influencing consumer purchasing decisions, particularly in this ever-changing innovative products context, studying how perceived risk affects consumers' information search behaviors among Chinese consumers has strong practical significance for Chinese innovation development.

A major implication originates from our findings is about how perceived risks, consumer innovativeness, demographic characteristics, and information searching behaviors of innovative products operate together. Based on what we found in the study, companies should provide targeted information to consumers, considering demographics and innate consumer innovativeness. For example, our findings show that for male consumers ongoing search, yet not pre-purchase search, is an important antecedent for their decision in learning about innovative products. The opposite is true for female consumers. According to the innovative product diffusion curve, the innovativeness levels of early adopters and subsequent users are not similar. Therefore, companies should focus on tailoring the information provided in marketing campaigns at various diffusion stages for innovative products.

Currently, Internet service providers seek to focus on all the complex antecedent conditions associated with the information search level by consumers. These configurations are likely to include recipes with a different level of perceived risk (functional risk and emotional risk)/innate consumer innovativeness/demographics. It is possible and worthwhile to identify these alternative complex conditions for theory and practice.

Limitations and Future Research

In this study, we used the self-report method, which may not reflect actual consuming situations. In the future, researchers could conduct similar studies using observational methods or process tracking tests to overcome this limitation. In addition, it is possible that for various types of innovative products consumers' perceived risks will differ as well as the effect of perceived risks on information search. In this study, we adopted the DSI scale to examine innate consumer innovativeness based on a specific product; however, consumer innovativeness and its moderating effect may vary with the type of product. Then, we use a tablet PC as the research stimulus. We encourage researchers to use other types of products as stimuli in future studies. Finally, we also encourage researchers to verify our results for non-innovative products or in countries other than China.

ACKNOWLEDGMENTS

The authors sincerely thank seminar participants at Center for Data-Driven Managerial Decision-Making.

FUNDING

This research is supported by the National Natural Science Foundation of China (Grants 71672038, 71428004) and The China Scholarship Council (Grant 201706105007).

REFERENCES

Barczak, G. 2012. "The Future of NPD/Innovation Research." *Journal of Product Innovation Management* 29 (3): 355–7. doi:10.1111/j.1540-5885.2012.00907.x.

Bettman, J. R. 1979. *An Information Processing Theory of Consumer Choice*. Reading, MA: Addison-Wesley Publishing Company.

Bettman, J. R., and C. W. Park. 1980. "Effect of Prior Knowledge and Experience and Phase of the Choice Process on Consumer Decision Process: A Protocol Analysis." *Journal of Consumer Research* 7 (3):234–48. doi:10.1086/208812.

Bloch, P. H., D. L. Sherrell, and N. M. Ridgway. 1986. "Consumer Search: An Extended Framework." *Journal of Consumer Research* 13 (1):119–26. doi:10.1086/209052.

Booz Allen Hamilton. 1982. *New Product Management for the 1980's*. New York, NY: Booz Allen Hamilton.

Brucks, M. 1985. "The Effects of Product Class Knowledge on Information Search Behavior." *Journal of Consumer Research* 12 (1):1–16. doi:10.1086/209031.

Center for Policy Alternatives. 1978. *Consumer Durables: Warranties, Service Contracts and Alternatives*. Boston, MA: Massachusetts Institute of Technology.

Chakravarti, A., and J. Xie. 2006. "Standards Competition and Effectiveness of Advertising Formats in New Product Introduction." *Journal of Marketing Research* 43 (2):224–36. doi:10.1509/jmkr.43.2.224.

Chaudhuri, A. 1997. "Consumption Emotion and Perceived Risk: A Macro-Analytic Approach." *Journal of Business Research* 39 (2):81–92. doi:10.1016/S0148-2963(96)00144-0.

Chaudhuri, A. 2000. "A Macro Analysis of the Relationship of Product Involvement and Information Search: The Role of Risk." *Journal of Marketing Theory and Practice* 8 (1):1–15. doi:10.1080/10696679.2000.11501856.

Claxton, J. D., J. N. Fry, and B. Portis. 1974. "A Taxonomy of Pre-Purchase Information Gathering Patterns." *Journal of Consumer Research* 1 (3):35–42. doi:10.1086/208598.

Conchar, M., G. M. Zinkhan, C. Peters, and S. Olavarrieta. 2004. "An Integrated Framework for the Conceptualization of Consumers' Perceived-Risk Processing." *Journal of the Academy of Marketing Science* 32 (4):418–36. doi:10.1177/0092070304267551.

Cowart, K. O., J. L. Fox, and A. E. Wilson. 2008. "A Structural Look at Consumer Innovativeness and Self-Congruence in New Product Purchases." *Psychology and Marketing* 25 (12):1111–30. doi:10.1002/mar.20256.

Cox, D. F. 1967. *Risk Taking and Information Handling in Consumer Behavior*. Boston, MA: Harvard University Press.

Dellaert, B. G. C., and G. Häubl. 2012. "Searching in Choice Mode: Consumer Decision Processes in Product Search with Recommendations." *Journal of Marketing Research* 49 (2):277–88. doi:10.1509/jmr.09.0481.

DeVellis, R. F. 2003. *Scale Development: Theory and Applications*. 2nd ed. Thousand Oaks, CA: Sage Publications.

Dholakia, U. M. 1998. "Involvement-Response Models of Joint Effects: An Empirical Test and Extension." *Advances in Consumer Research* 25 (1):499–506.

Dholakia, U. M. 2001. "A Motivational Process Model of Product Involvement and Consumer Risk Perception." *European Journal of Marketing* 35 (11/12):1340–60. doi:10.1108/EUM0000000006479.

Duşa, A. 2007. "User Manual for the QCA(GUI) Package in R." *Journal of Business Research* 60 (5):576–86. doi:10.1016/j.jbusres.2007.01.002.

Dwivedi, P., A. Joshi, and V. F. Misangyi. 2018. "Gender-Inclusive Gatekeeping: How (Mostly Male) Predecessors Influence the Success of Female CEOs." *Academy of Management Journal* doi:10.5465/amj.2015.1238.

Feurer, S., E. E. Baumbach, and A. G. Woodside. 2016. "Applying Configurational Theory to Build a Typology of Ethnocentric Consumers." *International Marketing Review* 33 (3):351–75. doi:10.1108/IMR-03-2014-0075.

Fiss, P. C. 2007. "A Set-Theoretic Approach to Organizational Configurations." *Academy of Management Review* 32 (4):1180–98. doi:10.5465/amr.2007.26586092.

Fiss, P. C. 2011. "Building Better Causal Theories: A Fuzzy Set Approach to Typologies in Organization Research." *Academy of Management Journal* 54 (2):393–420. doi:10.5465/amj.2011.60263120.

Garbarino, E., and M. Strahilevitz. 2004. "Gender Differences in the Perceived Risk of Buying Online and the Effects of Receiving a Site Recommendation." *Journal of Business Research* 57 (7):768–75. doi:10.1016/S0148-2963(02)00363-6.

Garcia-Castro, R., and C. Francoeur. 2016. "When More Is Not Better: Complementarities, Costs and Contingencies in Stakeholder Management." *Strategic Management Journal* 37 (2):406–24. doi:10.1002/smj.2341.

Gemunden, H. G. 1985. "Perceived Risk and Information Search: A Systematic Meta-Analysis of the Empirical Evidence." *International Journal of Research in Marketing* 2 (2):79–100.

Goldsmith, R. E., and V. Hofacker. 1991. "Measuring Consumer Innovativeness." *Journal of the Academy of Marketing Science* 19 (3):209–21. doi:10.1007/BF02726497.

Grandori, A., and S. Furnari. 2008. "A Chemistry of Organization: Combinatory Analysis and Design." *Organization Studies* 29 (3):459–85. doi:10.1177/0170840607088023.

Greckhamer, T. 2011. "Cross-Cultural Differences in Compensation Level and Inequality across Occupations: A Set-Theoretic Analysis." *Organization Studies* 32 (1):85–115. doi:10.1177/0170840610380806.

Hauser, J. R., and O. Toubia. 2005. "The Impact of Utility Balance and Endogeneity in Conjoint Analysis." *Marketing Science* 24 (3):498–507. doi:10.1287/mksc.1040.0108.

Hirschman, E. C. 1980. "Innovativeness, Novelty Seeking, and Consumer Creativity." *Journal of Consumer Research* 7 (3):283–95. doi:10.1086/208816.

Hirunyawipada, T., and A. K. Paswan. 2006. "Consumer Innovativeness and Perceived Risk: Implications for High Technology Product Adoption." *Journal of Consumer Marketing* 23 (4):333–58.

Hoffman, D. L., P. K. Kopalle, and T. P. Novak. 2010. "The "Right" Consumers for Better Concepts: Identifying Consumers High in Emergent Nature to Develop New Product Concepts." *Journal of Marketing Research* 47 (5): 854–65. doi:10.1509/jmkr.47.5.854.

Hoover, R. J., R. T. Green, and J. Saegert. 1978. "A Cross-National Study of Perceived Risk." *Journal of Marketing* 42 (3):102–8. doi:10.2307/1250543.

Hsiao, J. P., C. Jaw, T. C. Huan, and A. G. Woodside. 2015. "Applying Complexity Theory to Solve Hospitality Contrarian Case Conundrums: Illuminating Happy-Low and Unhappy-High Performing Frontline Service Employees." *International Journal of Contemporary Hospitality Management* 27 (4):608–47. doi:10.1108/IJCHM-11-2013-0533.

Huawei.com. 2015. "Huawei Watch." Available at: http://consumer.huawei.com/en/wearables/huawei-fit/index.htm

Im, S., B. L. Bayus, and C. H. Mason. 2003. "An Empirical Study of Innate Consumer Innovativeness, Personal Characteristics, and New-Product Adoption Behavior." *Journal of the Academy of Marketing Science* 31 (1): 61–73. doi:10.1177/0092070302238602.

Iyer, B., and T. H. Davenport. 2008. "Reverse Engineering Google's Innovation Machine." *Harvard Business Review* 86 (4):58–68.

Kaplan, Leon B., George J. Szybillo, and Jacob Jacoby. 1974. "Components of Perceived Risk in Product Purchase: A Cross Validation." *Journal of Applied Psychology* 59 (3):287–91. doi:10.1037/h0036657.

Kehoe, C., J. Pitkow, and K. Morton. 1998. "Eighth WWW User Survey." Available at: http://www.cc.gatech.edu/gvu/user_ surveys/survey-1998. (accessed on September 28, 2015).

Klink, R. R., and G. A. Athaide. 2010. "Consumer Innovativeness and the Use of New versus Extended Brand Names for New Products." *Journal of Product Innovation Management* 27 (1):23–32. doi:10.1111/j.1540-5885.2009.00697.x.

Kirton, M. 1976. "Adaptors and Innovators: A Description and Measure." *Journal of Applied Psychology* 61 (5): 622–9. doi:10.1037/0021-9010.61.5.622.

Kotler, P., and K. L. Keller. 2012. *Marketing Management*. 14th ed. New York, NY: Prentice Hall.

Lee, S., J. H. Lee, and T. C. Garrett. 2013. "A Study of the Attitude toward Convergent Products: A Focus on the Consumer Perception of Functionalities." *Journal of Product Innovation Management* 30 (1):123–35. doi:10.1111/j.1540-5885.2012.00991.x.

Levav, J., N. Reinholtz, and C. Lin. 2012. "The Effect of Ordering Decisions by Choice-Set Size on Consumer Search." *Journal of Consumer Research* 39 (3):585–99. doi:10.1086/664498.

Li, G., R. Zhang, and C. Wang. 2015. "The Role of Product Originality, Usefulness and Motivated Consumer Innovativeness in New Product Adoption Intentions." *Journal of Product Innovation Management* 32 (2):214–23. doi:10.1111/jpim.12169.

Midgley, D. F., and G. R. Dowling. 1978. "Innovativeness: The Concept and Its Measurement." *Journal of Consumer Research* 4 (4):229–42. doi:10.1086/208701.

Mitchell, V. M. 1999. "Consumer Perceived Risk: Conceptualizations and Models." *European Journal of Marketing* 33 (1/2):163–95. doi:10.1108/03090569910249229.

Mitchell, V. W. 2001. "Re-Conceptualizing Consumer Store Image Processing Using Perceived Risk." *Journal of Business Research* 54 (2):167–72. doi:10.1016/S0148-2963(99)00086-7.

Mitra, K., M. C. Reiss, and L. M. Capella. 1999. "An Examination of Perceived Risk, Information Search and Behavioral Intentions in Search, Experience and Credence Services." *Journal of Services Marketing* 13 (3): 208–28. doi:10.1108/08876049910273763.

Miyazaki, A. D., and A. Fernandez. 2001. "Consumer Perceptions of Privacy and Security Risks for Online Shopping." *Journal of Consumer Affairs* 35 (1):27–44. doi:10.1111/j.1745-6606.2001.tb00101.x.

Murray, K. B. 1991. "A Test of Services Marketing Theory: Consumer Information Acquisition Activities." *Journal of Marketing* 55 (1):11–25.

Murray, K. B., and J. L. Schlacter. 1990. "The Impact of Services versus Goods on Consumer's Assessment of Perceived Risk and Variability." *Journal of the Academy of Marketing Science* 18 (1):51–65. doi:10.1007/BF02729762.

Norden, L., C. S. Buston, and W. Wagner. 2014. "Financial Innovation and Bank Behavior: Evidence from Credit Markets." *Journal of Economic Dynamics and Control* 43:130–45. doi:10.1016/j.jedc.2014.01.015.

PDMA. 2017. "Product Development & Management Association." Available at: http://www.pdma.org.

Peter, J. P., and M. J. Ryan. 1976. "An Investigation of Perceived Risk at the Brand Level." *Journal of Marketing Research* 13 (2):184–8. doi:10.1177/002224377601300210.

Pham, M. T., and H. H. Chang. 2010. "Regulatory Focus, Regulatory Fit, and the Search and Consideration of Choice Alternatives." *Journal of Consumer Research* 37 (4):626–40. doi:10.1086/655668.

Phillips, L. W., and B. Sternthal. 1977. "Age Differences in Information Processing: A Perspective on the Aged Consumer." *Journal of Marketing Research* 14 (4):444–57. doi:10.1177/002224377701400402.

Ragin, C. C. 1997. "Turning the Tables: How Case-Oriented Methods Challenge Variable Oriented Methods." *Comparative Social Research* 16 (1):27–42.

Ragin, C. C. 2000. *Fuzzy-Set Social Science*. Chicago, IL: University of Chicago Press.

Ragin, C. C. 2006. *User's Guide to Fuzzy-Set/Qualitative Comparative Analysis 2.0*. Tucson, AZ: Department of Sociology, University of Arizona.

Ragin, C. C. 2008. *Redesigning Social Inquiry: Fuzzy Sets and Beyond*. Chicago, IL: University of Chicago Press.

Ragin, C. C., K. A. Drass, and S. Davey. 2006. *Fuzzy-Set/Qualitative Comparative Analysis 2.0*. Tucson, AZ: Department of Sociology, University of Arizona.

Ragin, C. C., and P. C. Fiss. 2009. "Net Effects Analysis versus Configurational Analysis: An Empirical Demonstration." In *Redesigning Social Inquiry: Set Relations in Social Research*, edited by C. C. Ragin, 190–212. Chicago, IL: University of Chicago Press.

Roselius, T. 1971. "Consumer Ranking of Risk Reduction Methods." *Journal of Marketing* 35 (1):56–61. doi:10.1177/002224297103500110.

Roth, E., J. Seong, and J. Woetzel. 2015. "Gauging the Strength of Chinese Innovation." October, Accessed https://www.mckinsey.com.

Solomon, M. R. 2012. *Consumer Behavior*. 10th ed. Englewood Cliffs, NJ: Prentice Hall.

Spence, H. E., J. F. Engel, and R. D. Blackwell. 1970. "Perceived Risk in Mail-Order and Retail Store Buying." *Journal of Marketing Research* 7 (3):364–9. doi:10.1177/002224377000700313.

Srinivasan, N., and B. T. Ratchford. 1991. "An Empirical Test of a Model of External Search for Automobiles." *Journal of Consumer Research* 18 (2):233–42. doi:10.1086/209255.

Stone, R. N., and K. Gronhaug. 1993. "Perceived Risk: Further Considerations for the Marketing Discipline." *European Journal of Marketing* 27 (3):39–50. doi:10.1108/03090569310026637.

Urry, J. 2005. "The Complexity Turn." *Theory Culture and Society* 22 (5):1–14. doi:10.1177/0263276405057188.

Vandecasteele, B., and M. Geuens. 2010. "Motivated Consumer Innovativeness: Concept, Measurement, and Validation." *International Journal of Research in Marketing* 27 (4):308–18. doi:10.1016/j.ijresmar.2010.08.004.

Woetzel, J., Y. Chen, J. Manyika, E. Roth, J. Seong, and J. Lee. 2015. "The China Effect on Global Innovation." October, Accessed https://www.mckinsey.com.

Woodside, A. G. 2014. "Embrace Perform Model: Complexity Theory, Contrarian Case Analysis, and Multiple Realities." *Journal of Business Research* 67 (12):2495–503. doi:10.1016/j.jbusres.2014.07.006.

Wu, P. L., S. S. Yeh, T. C. Huan, and A. G. Woodside. 2014. "Applying Complexity Theory to Deepen Service Dominant Logic: Configurational Analysis of Customer Experience-and-Outcome Assessments of Professional Services for Personal Transformations." *Journal of Business Research* 67 (8):1647–70. doi:10.1016/j.jbusres.2014.03.012.

Zuckerman, Z. 2013. "Innovation is About Behavior, Not Products." http://www.inc.com

Success Factors for Product Innovation in China's Manufacturing Sector: Strategic Choice and Environment Constraints

Zhenzhong Ma (iD) and Quan Jin (iD)

Abstract: This study examines what factors contribute to firm innovation performance as a result of successful launch of new products in China. Rather than simply applying theories of product innovation often developed in the West, this study takes an indigenous perspective to explore what product strategies and which environment factors, defined by Chinese managers, contribute to the improved firm performance. With the data of Chinese firms from over 40 cities across the country, this study surveys more than 700 manufacturing firms that have introduced new products to the market. The result shows that while a defensive product strategy is negatively related to a firm's patent application, a prospector strategy helps increase its market share in China. In addition, innovation policy and total R&D investment drive a firm to sell more products overseas and increase its new product sales across the globe. Local talent market can also help improve a firm's patent application but often drive the firm to focus more on domestic markets. Implications of the results for theory and practice are discussed.

INTRODUCTION

Product innovation is a key to a firm's survival and growth. Successful launch of new products can have positive impact on the firm's performance (Beers and Zand 2014; Dahlander, O'Mahony, and Gann 2016; Di Benedetto 1999; Dibrell, Craig, and Neubaum 2014; Fréchet and Goy 2017; Ma et al. 2015; Zhang, Hu, and Kotabe 2011). Empirical studies have pointed to high failure rates of new product launch in the market (Dahlander, O'Mahony, and Gann 2016; Ernst 2002; Parry and Song, 1994; Sirén and Kohtamäki 2016). It is, therefore, crucial for managers to better understand the factors that impact the success of new products.

Identifying such success factors has become the objective of most studies in product development and innovation success (Beers and Zand 2014; Calantone Schmidt, and Song 1996; Dahlander, O'Mahony, and Gann 2016; Ernst, 2002; Ettlie and Subramaniam 2004).

Given its direct relevance and inherent appeal, product innovation and development research has been able to retain a high level of popularity among scholars over the last three decades (Dahlander, O'Mahony, and Gann 2016; Ernst 2002; Ma et al. 2015). A large number of studies have explored the factors that may facilitate new product success in different sectors from different perspectives (e.g., Beers and Zand 2014; Calantone, Chan, and Cui 2006; Dyer and Song 1998; Ernst 2002; Fréchet and Goy 2017; Lichtenthaler and Ernst 2007; Ma et al. 2015; Subramaniam and Venkatraman 2001). However, in comparison with the tremendous amount of research on product innovation and new product development in the West, relatively little has been done in the context of China (Ernst 2002; Ma et al. 2015; Zhang, Hu, and Kotabe 2011), one of the most important emerging markets that has the potential to become next economic super power with its world second largest GDP and fastest economic growth.

Along with its three-decade-long transition to a market economy, China has undergone massive restructuring of its innovation system. China's economy and technology have, thus, experienced astounding growth in the last two decades, and China has gained a reputation as the "world's factory." Moreover, China has also aspired to become the world's innovation center. In particular, China has initiated a number of national programs to reform its innovation system since the 1980s and has, thus, experienced science and technology take-off since the middle of 1990s. In 2006, China further announced its "Guideline for the National Medium- and Long-term Science and Technology Development Programs (2006–2020)," the focus of which is to highlight the strategic role of innovation and to lay out a number of goals and specific measures in order to boost China's aspiration to become an innovation center by 2020 (Ma et al. 2015; Ma, Lee, and Chen 2009). China's Premier, Li Keqiang, has called recently for "mass entrepreneurship and innovation" to achieve a "better-quality, more efficient, upgraded economy" (2015). Therefore, a good understanding of product innovation and new product development in China has the potential to help better understand the emerging trends in product innovation in the global context. It may also help understanding the rising of the emerging markets multinationals, which are sure to become formidable competitors of the multinationals from developed countries.

This study adopts an institutional view to explore new trends in product innovation by examining the impact of strategic choice and environment constraints on product innovation and new product development. The findings of this study have the potential to demonstrate how successful launch of new products can improve overall firm performance, as measured by patent applications, global and domestic sales, and market shares. While research on product innovation in the West has produced an impressive list of success factors in product innovation and new product development (Ernst, 2002; Fréchet and Goy, 2017; Song et al. 2011; Souder and Song, 1997, 1998; Subramaniam, 2006; Subramaniam, Rosenthal, and Hatten, 1998), it is not very clear whether these factors may make the same impact in China too (Ma et al. 2015; Song and Parry 1994; Xie, Song, and Stringfellow 2003; Zhang, Hu, and Kotabe 2011). This study adopts an indigenous perspective to investigate the success factors in product innovation in China, and the impacts of these factors in the eyes of Chinese managers.

There is also lack of research that specifically examines China's unique environmental constraints, namely, the institutional context that might strongly affect manufacturing firms' performance in the process of product innovation. China has a dramatically different institutional system where there are many cultural and social barriers that make it very difficult, or even impossible, to simply apply the success factors identified in the West to the Chinese market (Chua, Roth, and Lemoine 2015; Ma et al. 2015; Song and Chen 2014; Song and Parry 1994). This study is a powerful test of the universalistic application of western theory in product innovation in China. An examination of the impact of strategic choice and environmental constraints on product innovation and firm performance in China helps explore the unique characteristics of the Chinese market, thereby facilitating the entrance of multinational corporations from developed countries into the Chinese market.

Conceptual Framework

The continuous development and market introduction of new products is an important determinant of firm performance (Beers and Zand 2014; Dibrell, Craig, and Neubaum 2014; Ernst 2002). The studies of the factors that enhance introduction of new products have gained great significance, and scholars have explored various success factors from different perspectives (Ernst 2002), such as a resource-based perspective (Kamasak 2015), a resource-advantage perspective (Song and Chen 2014), and an institutional perspective (Ma et al. 2015). An impressive array of literature, thus, has been generated on product innovation and its associated antecedents and effect factors (e.g., Beers and Zand 2014; Cooper and Kleinschmidt 1995a, 1996; Di Benedetto 1999; Dyer and Song 1998; Ernst 2002; Fréchet and Goy 2017; Sirén and Kohtamäki 2016; Song and Montoya-Weiss 2001; Song and Noh 2006; Song, Song, and Di Benedetto 2009; Souder and Song 1997, 1998; Subramaniam, Rosenthal, and Hatten 1998).

The majority of the research on product innovation in the past decades has focused on the economics of new product development, effects of market orientation on product innovation, practitioner-oriented normative how-to approaches in product development and innovation, the innovation adoption process, and the descriptive, yet generally anecdotal, firm characteristics that serve to generate innovation (Dahlander, O'Mahony, and Gann 2016; Ernst 2002; Fréchet and Goy 2017; Pullen et al. 2009; Siguaw, Simpson, and Enz 2006; Song and Chen 2014). The empirical literature on new product development and innovation has shown that the presence of a product development and innovation process creates the basis for the success of new product innovation, and within this process, the quality of planning, the necessary preparatory work, the rough evaluation of the product innovation ideas, and the execution of the technical and economic feasibility studies are decisive in new product development and innovation (Dibrell, Craig, and Neubaum 2014; Ernst 2002; Fréchet and Goy 2017; Sirén and Kohtamäki 2016).

According to institutional theory, organizations operating in varying institutional environments will face diverse environmental pressures, and organizations must adapt to their environment with proper competitive strategies in order to survive and thrive (Scott 2008). Social, economic, and political factors constitute a particular institutional environment that provides firms with advantages for engaging in specific types of activities there, such as a particular set of product innovations strategies or new product development plans. As such, it is contended that firm strategies and their environmental constraints affect firm performance (DiMaggio and Powell 1983; Scott 2008).

Based on the notion that firm strategy and environment constraints jointly determine firm performance (Dibrell, Craig, and Neubaum 2014; Fréchet and Goy 2017; Ma et al. 2015; Prescott 1986; Sirén and Kohtamäki 2016), scholars have identified and examined a number of factors for their possible impact on, or correlations with, the success of product innovation and development (see Ernst 2002; Ma et al. 2015; Siguaw, Simpson, and Enz 2006 for a review). For example, a meta-analysis has found that new product development and innovation process, organization of product development projects, organizational culture, commitment of senior management, and the strategy of product innovation and development can greatly improve the chance of success in new product development and product innovation (Beers and Zand 2014; Ernst 2002).

In addition, environmental factors that define the setting where new products are developed or innovated are found to affect the process and further the success of new product development (Cooper and Kleinschmidt 1995b; Song and Chen 2014; Song and Parry 1994; Song et al. 2010, 2011). Specific environmental factors that have been examined and found relevant to product innovation include the market where new products compete, the compatibility of new products with the firm's existing skills, the specific characteristics of new product innovation, and the needs of the market and the customers (Ernst 2002; Song and Chen 2014).

However, while a great deal of research has explored product innovation and its success factors, and a large number of success factors have also been identified in the product innovation literature, current empirical studies on product innovation and new product development have largely focused on technical contents of product innovation and, somehow, ignored the big strategic picture (Dibrell, Craig, and Neubaum 2014: Ernst 2002; Ma et al. 2015). Often, a battery of single items are used as independent or dependent variables and tested for their relationships with bivariate testing procedures, which then result in a flood of confusing findings, depending on what variables are used in the studies (Ernst 2002). Consequently, it is extremely difficult to observe the "product innovation" forest among myriad "results" trees (Brown and Eisenhardt 1995; Fréchet and Goy 2017). In particular, strategic choices and environment constraints jointly affect firm performance (Dibrell, Craig, and Neubaum 2014; Fréchet and Goy 2017; Ma et al. 2015; Prescott 1986), and the construct of new product strategy is identified as the second most important success factors for new product development (Cooper and Kleinschmidt 1995b; Ernst 2002). Yet, the product development and innovation strategy has rarely been examined in product innovation research in the past three decades (Ernst 2002; Fréchet and Goy 2017), with only a few notable exceptions (e.g., DeSarbo et al. 2005; Fréchet and Goy 2017; Gatignon and Xuereb 1997; Griffin 1997; Guan et al. 2009; Song et al. 2011).

Strategic choice is considered very important in product innovation because a strategic framework offers orientation to the sum of individual product innovation projects, provides a long-term thrust, and thus goes beyond the completion of short- or even medium-term product innovation projects (Fréchet and Goy 2017; Sirén and Kohtamäki 2016; Song and Chen 2014). Given its positive influence on product innovation, the product innovation strategy deserves more research attention. The relationship between product innovation strategy and overall product innovation performance should be carefully examined in order to identify the best practices in new product launch (Fréchet and Goy 2017; Ma et al. 2015; Sirén and Kohtamäki 2016).

Globalization and increasing market uncertainty in the world market also require examination of product innovation success factors in an international context, especially when multinationals have built strong existence, often in the form of international joint ventures across the globe. According to institutional theory, organizations must conform to the rules and belief systems prevailing in the institutional context in order to compete in that environment for survival and growth (DiMaggio and Powell 1983; Scott 2008). There is substantial evidence that firms in different types of economic systems react differently to similar challenges (Scott 2008). The institutional environment provides organizations with advantages for engaging in specific types of activities. Organizations tend to perform better when they receive institutional support (Scott 2008).

Multinational corporations (MNCs) operating in a number of countries face diverse institutional pressures. These pressures exert fundamental influences on their product innovation and new product development strategies. Thus, in order to remain competitive international managers must understand success factors in product innovation in different institutional contexts (Song, Di Benedetto, and Zhao 1999; Song and Chen 2014). A better understanding of the relationship between strategic choices, environmental constraints, and product innovation in various local contexts becomes one of the most important sources of global competitive advantage (Fréchet and Goy 2017; Dibrell, Craig, and Neubaum 2014; Song and Parry 1996; 1997a, 1997b; Song, Kawakami, and Stringfellow 2010; Song et al. 2011). Identifying those factors that influence product innovation in the international context becomes crucially important to researchers and managers.

Guided by institutional theory-based framework, the current study examines the impact of strategic choice and institutional constraints on the performance of product innovation in China's manufacturing sector, using an indigenous perspective in order to explore the key success factors for product innovation in the eyes of Chinese managers. With respect to strategic choice, this study adopts the framework of organization strategies developed by Miles and Snow's (1978) to consider two typical strategies: defender strategy and prospector strategy. In this study, it is expected that firms that apply defensive product innovation strategy (defender) are more reactive to changes in the market, often have a limited range of products, and focus on efficiency and process improvement to protect their market. Firms with a prospective product innovation strategy (prospector) have a broad product spectrum and often lead the market in product innovation by trying to launch new products and entering new markets ahead of their competitors (Miles and Snow 1978). Therefore, it is hypothesized as follows:

>H1a: *A firm's defender strategy in new product development is negatively related to product innovation performance.*

>H1b: *A firm's* prospector *strategy in new product development is positively related to product innovation performance.*

This study examines typical factors often used to discuss institutional environment and their impact on product innovation, including innovation policy, government regulation and infrastructure, professional services, and talent market (Ma et al. 2015; Grewal and Dharwadkar 2002). R&D investment, as an important determining factor for product innovation, reflects how firms invest to improve their research and development activities, a critical part of their product innovation efforts, and thus, it is also examined for its impact on product innovation. The explorative research hypothesis tested in this study is the belief that strategic choice and the environment relevant to product innovation affect firm performance in China's manufacturing sector. It is, thus, hypothesized as follows:

>H2a: *Conducive innovation policy is positively related to product innovation performance.*

>H2b: *Supportive government regulations are positively related to product innovation performance.*

>H2c: *Well-developed infrastructure is positively related to product innovation performance.*

>H2d: *Quality professional services are positively related to product innovation performance.*

>H2e: *Rich talent market is positively related to product innovation performance.*

>H2f: *Rate of R&D investment is positively related to product innovation performance.*

In addition, instead of simply testing the applicability of the measures developed in the West in the Chinese context, and unlike many other studies that often focus on the technical contents of product innovation, this study develops scales based on the responses from local Chinese managers in their assessing product innovation performance to measure strategic choice and environment factors considered important. This study, then, investigates the question of what product strategies and what environment factors facilitate the improvement of firm performance as a whole, rather than the success of a single product innovation project. The indigenous approach to product innovation and strategic choice and environment constraints helps refining product innovation theory developed in the West. It also helps moving forward the process of building a more robust theory on product innovation and new product development in the increasingly globalized world market (Dibrell, Craig, and Neubaum 2014; Fréchet and Goy 2017; Ma et al. 2015; Song and Parry 1994, 1996, 1997a, 1997b; Zhang, Hu, and Kotabe 2011).

METHODS

Data Collection Instrument

This study takes an indigenous perspective to explore how strategic choice and environment constraints affect a firm's product innovation performance. All the scales used in this study are developed from interviews with Chinese managers focusing on their understanding of product innovation strategy and environment issues that may affect product innovation and overall firm performance. The language of all the questionnaires used in this study was Chinese.

To begin with, we compiled a list of items on product innovation strategy and environment factors from past success studies on product innovation and new product development (Cooper and Kleinschmidt 1995a, 1996; Guan et al. 2009; Parry and Song 1994; Song and Parry 1994; Zhang, Hu, and Kotabe 2011). We conducted the study in ten well-known Chinese manufacturing firms, including Huawei, Lenovo, ZTE, Irico Group, Konka Group, Galanz Group, Wanxiang Group, Hansteel Group, Aviation Industry Corporation of China, and Tangsteel Group. We conducted semi-structured interviews with 45 senior managers in these firms and, further, consulted with six management scholars before we created a questionnaire for this study.

The questionnaire was first pretested in 45 manufacturing enterprises by asking their senior managers to evaluate whether the items included in the questionnaire were complete and appropriate for assessing their product innovation strategies and environmental factors that have affected their product development and innovation process. The questionnaire was, then, adjusted based on the pretest results to improve its construct validity. The final questionnaire includes the measures for the dependent variables--patent application, domestic market share, external orientation, global new product sales, and domestic new product sales, and the independent variables--defender strategy, prospector strategy, innovation policy, government regulations, infrastructure, professional services, talent market, and R&D investment. Detailed explanations of these variables follow.

Product Innovation Strategy. The resulting questionnaire for strategic choice consists of ten items, and respondents are asked to indicate on a 5-point Likert scale the extent to which they agree or disagree with a given statement describing their product innovation strategy in the past three years, with 1 representing "Strongly Disagree" and 5 "Strongly Agree". Sample items include "In creating innovation strategy, priority is given to product innovation rather than procedural innovation" and "In product innovation, priority is given to those that can reduce costs, rather than to developing niche products" (see Table 1).

Environmental Factors. The environment factors consist of 22 different issues that are considered important by the well-known manufacturing firms and the pretested firms in affecting product innovation processes. Respondents are asked to indicate on a 5-point Likert scale how a given environmental factor affects their product innovation in the past three years, with 1 representing "Very Negative" and 5 "Very Positive." Sample items include "Government's restriction on product prices," "Government's innovation policies," and "Protection of intellectual property rights" (see Table 2). In addition, R&D investment, as an

TABLE 1
Factor Analysis of Product Innovation Strategies in China's Manufacturing Enterprises

	Factor Loading	
Variable Items	1	2
Prospector Strategy		
1. In product innovation, priority is given to entering new industries, rather than strengthening the present business.	0.79	
2. In R&D investment, priority is given to developing new markets and technological innovation.	0.77	
3. Wait for better opportunities rather than act right away, in face of radical change in industry technologies (reverse code)	0.66	
4. In product innovation, priority is given to improving firm expansion and market share, rather than strengthening the present business	0.59	
5. Priority is given to product innovation rather than procedural innovation.	0.45	
Defender Strategy		
1. When new products from other companies are introduced to the market, priority is given to imitating these products to reduce the gap, rather than developing new niche products.		0.77
2. In R&D, priority is given to research on applied technology, rather than basic research.		0.76
3. In product innovation, priority is given to those that can reduce costs, rather than to developing niche products.		0.58
Variance (%)	29.1	22.3
Eigen values	2.83	1.28

important source of competitive advantage, was also included in the questionnaire to assess the extent to which the manufacturing firms try to improve their research and development activities, a critical part of their product innovation efforts.

Firm Performance. The measures for firm performance focused on the economic aspects, mainly because they are the ultimate criterion variables in management research (Ernst 2002). These measures include global and domestic sales brought by the innovated new products (global new product sales and domestic new product sales), domestic market share, external orientation, and total patent application. Global new product sales assess the total overseas sales of the innovated products as a percentage of the firm's total sales, and domestic new product sales assess the new innovated product sales in China's market as a

TABLE 2
Factor Analysis of Environment Constraints for Product Innovation in China

Variable Items	Factor Loading				
	1	2	3	4	5
Government Regulations					
1. Government's restrictions on a firm's business areas.	0.81				
2. Government's restriction on purchase/bidding from the firm.	0.78				
3. Government's restriction on product prices.	0.77				
4. Ownership-based government restriction and local protectionism.	0.77				
Innovation Policy					
1. Government's innovation policies.		0.77			
2. Protection of intellectual property rights.		0.69			
3. Taxation and legal policies for innovation.		0.60			
4. Local universities and research institutes for innovation.		0.59			
5. Government's policy on purchase innovative products.		0.56			
6. Industrial rules and regulations		0.54			
7. Banking and financial policies for product innovation.		0.47			
Infrastructure					
1. Telecommunication, transportation, logistics, and others.			0.76		
2. Education, medical services and other public services.			0.74		
3. Living conditions.			0.70		
4. Social and cultural environment.			0.68		
Professional Service					
1. Professional business services.				0.82	
2. Professional technical services.				0.82	
Talent Market					
1. Senior technological professional talent market.					0.89
2. Senior management professional talent market.					0.88
Variance (%)	34.93	11.14	7.17	6.29	5.69
Eigen values	6.64	2.12	1.36	1.20	1.08

percentage of the firm's total sales. Domestic market share measures the firm's market share ranking in China's market, while external orientation assesses the firm's overseas product market as a percentage of its total market.

Total patent application as a result of product innovation is also included to measure firm performance. Patent statistics as a measure of innovative activities' output and technological strength has been widely accepted (Ma and Lee 2008) because patent information is publicly available and provides very specific and detailed information for tracing innovative activities over time. Researchers often favor patent information and use it as a robust measure of product and technological innovation performance. In the study, all the scores for the dependent variables and independent variables were provided by the surveyed managers.

Firm Sampling

The data for the main study was collected with the assistance of the National Bureau of Statistics of China (NBSC) between 2008 and 2010 in 40 cities across China. With a preliminary screening process on the data available at the NBSC, a total of 1,409 manufacturing firms were randomly selected by using a stratified random sampling method. The companies were contacted to find out whether they have launched new products in the past three years and whether they agree to participate in this study. This exercise resulted in identifying over 700 publicly listed firms that have launched new products or conducted product innovation activities. They voluntarily participated in this study. State-owned enterprises and non-publicly listed companies in the private sectors were excluded from the analysis since very few of them had launched new products within the study's timeframe. It is possible that state owned enterprises' lack in flexibility and private companies' lack in resources were the reasons for their or low rate of product innovation.

The final database consisted of 725 manufacturing firms from various fields; 35 percent of the participating firms have 300 or less employees, 48.1 percent of the companies have between 300 and 2,000 employees, and the rest of the companies employ over 2,000 employees. The majority of the participating firms have a total asset between RMB 40 million and 400 million (about 51%) in 2007. About 34 percent of them have a total asset larger than RMB 400 million. The distribution of their total sales in 2007 were less than RMB 30 million (11.3%), between RMB 30 million and 300 million (44.7%), and over 300 RMB (44%) (see Table 3).

The respondents from each participating firm were general managers or the corresponding department heads of production and financial departments, who were knowledgeable about their companies' innovative activities and corresponding firm performance. All 725 firms were used in the analysis that explored the research question developed in the earlier section of this article, namely, how strategic choice and institutional constraints affect general firm's performance as a result of aggregated product innovation activities in China's manufacturing sector?

RESULTS

In this study, we first factor analyzed the strategic choice and environment constraint issues in order to have a better understanding of key success factors in product innovation and their impact on firm performance. The factor analysis of issues related to strategic choice, with the principal component, varimax rotation method, and after two items of the original questionnaire were deleted from the analysis due to their low factor loadings, it yielded two factors. The first factor is titled "prospective product innovation strategy," and the second factor is titled "defensive product innovation strategy." Together they accounted for about 52 percent of the variance. Consistent with the notion of Miles and Snow's (1978) typology of organizational strategy, firms with a prospective product innovation strategy (prospector) have a broad product domain and often lead the change in product innovation and try to launch new products and enter new markets ahead of their competitors. This factor includes five items, with a reliability alpha coefficient of 0.71. Firms that apply defensive product innovation strategy (defender) are more reactive in their response to change in products and market, and often have a limited range of products and focus on efficiency and process improvement

TABLE 3
Sample Composition

Firm Type	Number of Firms	Percentage of Sample
Firm Size		
300 employees or less	254	35.0%
300–2000 employees in total	349	48.1%
2000 employees or more	122	16.9%
Total	725	100 %
Total Sales (RMB Million)		
Less than 30	82	11.3%
Between 30 and 300	324	44.7%
Over 300	319	44.0%
Total	725	100 %
Total Assets (RMB Million)		
Less than 40	109	15.0%
Between 40 and 400	372	51.3%
Over 400	244	33.7%
Total	725	100 %
Firm Type		
Agricultural food and processing	24	3.3
Industrial Food	20	2.8
Soft drinks	10	1.4
Tobacco	5	0.7
Textile	39	5.4
Textile-based clothes, shoes, and caps manufacturer	23	3.2
Fur, leather, feather processing and clothes	5	0.7
Wood processing, and wood, bamboo and other related products	11	1.5
Furniture	5	0.7
Paper and paper products	9	1.2
Printing and printing media	8	1.1
Stationary and sports equipment manufacturer	3	0.4
Gasoline processing and related products	10	1.4
Chemicals and chemical-based products	45	6.2
Medicine	39	5.4
Chemical fiber	10	1.4
Rubber	7	1.0
Plastic products	23	3.2
Non-metal mineral products	31	4.3
Ferrous metal processing	29	4.0
Non-ferrous metal processing	29	4.0
Metal Products	45	6.2
General equipment manufacturer	31	4.3
Special equipment manufacturer	62	8.6
Transportation equipment	61	8.4
Machinery for manufacturing electric equipment	37	5.1
Telecommunication equipment, computers, and other electronics	63	8.7
Measuring instruments and machinery for culture and office	11	1.5
Crafts and other product manufacturer	28	3.9
Waste recycling	2	0.3
Total	725	100%

(Miles and Snow 1978). This factor includes three items, with a reliability alpha coefficient of 0.60 (see Tables 1 and 4).

We also used the principal component analysis with varimax rotation method to factor analyze the issues on environmental constraints. After deleting three items from the original questionnaire due to their low factor loadings, five environment factors emerged and together they accounted for about 65.1% of the variance. Based on their annotations, these factors were given descriptive names as follows: (1) government regulations, which include a variety of government policies and restrictions on firms regarding their businesses and product domains (four items, reliability of the alpha coefficient of 0.84); (2) innovation policies, which include different policies and protections that are directly related to a firm's product innovation and research and development efforts (seven items, reliability alpha coefficient of 0.83); (3) infrastructure, which assesses different aspects of environmental hardware and software, such as transportation and telecommunication (four items, reliability alpha coefficient of 0.78); (4) professional service, which assesses the extent to which different professional services are available for product innovation and relevant efforts including local business services and technical services (two items, reliability alpha coefficient of 0.80); and (5) talent market, which measures the market of both professional technical talents and management talents available for recruitment (two items, reliability alpha coefficient of 0.88) (see Tables 2 and 4). The descriptive statistics of all the variables and their bivariate correlations are reported in Table 4.

To test the main impact of strategic choice and environment constraints on overall firm performance as the sum of all product innovation activities, the criterion variables were regressed respectively on the independent variables. These included two types of product innovation strategies, five different environment constraints, and total R&D investment. The relationship was controlled for the effects of firm's size, total assets, and total sales. We also tested the possible multicollinearity among all variables. The variance inflation factors (VIFs) are all below 2, indicating that multicollinearity was not a problem. The final regression results are shown in Table 5 and Figure 1.

The regression results show that, as expected, both strategic choice and environment constraints have significant influence on firm performance. More specifically, the firms with a defensive strategy tend to have less patent applications, an important output indicator of innovation activities, while the firms that adopted a prospector strategy were found to be more likely to gain higher domestic market share in China, in support of H1a and H1b. With respect to environmental factors, it is found that innovation policy is an important firm's performance driver, which has a positive and significant relationship with both global new product sales and overseas market share as a percentage of a firm's total market (external orientation), in support of H2a. While neither government regulations nor infrastructure is found to be significantly related to any of the criterion variables of firm's performance (thus neither H2b nor H2c is supported), local talent market, or the availability of local technical and management talents, is found to help improve a firm's total patent application. At the same time, it also reduces the firm's effort to increase overseas market share. Both business services and technical services are found to be positively related to the firm's domestic new product sales, in support of H2d and H2e.

TABLE 4

Means, Standard Deviations, and Correlations.

Variables	Mean	SD	1	2	3	4	5	6	7	8	9	10	11	12	13	14	15	16
1. Firm Size	1.82	0.70	–															
2. Total Assets	2.19	0.67	0.68***	–														
3. Total Sales	2.34	0.66	0.62***	0.78***	-													
4. Defender Strategy	3.52	0.50	0.12**	0.08*	0.09*	(0.60)												
5. Prospector Strategy	3.36	0.69	0.01	–0.01	–0.06	0.38***	(0.71)											
6. Innovation Policy	3.46	0.55	0.07*	0.15***	0.11**	0.03	0.13***	(0.83)										
7. Government Regulations	3.10	0.60	–0.03	0.04	0.00	–0.03	0.11**	0.52***	(0.84)									
8. Infrastructure	3.35	0.57	–0.03	0.05	0.08*	0.05	0.12**	0.48***	0.31***	(0.78)								
9. Professional Service	3.20	0.59	–0.01	0.07*	0.08*	–0.04	0.07	0.51***	0.26***	0.46***	(0.80)							
10. Talent Market	3.25	0.86	–0.03	0.03	0.08*	–0.02	0.13***	0.43***	0.25***	0.42***	0.40***	(0.88)						
11. R&D Investment	0.02	1.13	0.17***	0.13**	0.10*	0.04	0.02	0.02	–0.00	0.01	0.05	–0.01	-					
12. Total Patent Application	16.9	78.0	0.19***	0.17***	0.14***	–0.06	–0.03	0.05	–0.02	0.05	–0.01	0.04	0.09*	-				
13. Domestic Market Share	3.58	1.47	–0.26***	–0.30***	–0.26***	0.01	0.07	–0.09*	0.02	0.01	0.02	0.06	–0.11*	–0.16***	-			
14. External Orientation	2.08	1.08	0.28***	0.24***	0.18***	0.03	0.04	0.12*	0.06	0.00	0.04	–0.04	0.16***	0.13***	–0.25***	-		
15. Global New Prod Sales (%)	12.4	21.2	0.07	0.08	0.07	–0.09	0.06	0.19***	0.08	0.06	0.11	0.15*	0.22***	0.05	–0.16*	0.24***	-	
16. Domestic New Prod Sales (%)	30.3	27.9	–0.08	0.05	0.05	–0.00	0.04	0.12*	0.01	0.05	0.03	0.04	0.07	0.02	–0.11*	0.02	0.05	-

Note: Total sample size $N = 725$; firm size $N = 300$ employees or below, $2 = 300–2,000$, $3 = 2,000$ or above; total sales: $1 = $ RMB 30 million or below, $2 = $ RMB 30 million to 300 million, $3 = $ RMB 300 million or above; total assets: $1 = $ RMB 40 million or below, $2 = $ RMB 40 million to 400 million, $3 = $ RMB 400 million or above; corporate product strategies and environment factors are based on 5-point Likert scales; total R&D investments are standardized scores; domestic market share is based on a firm's market share ranking: $1 = $ No. 1 in market share, $2 = $ No. 2–5 in market share, $3 = $ No. 6–10 in market share, $4 = $ No. 11–50, and $5 = $ No. 50+. The numbers in bold along the diagonal line are reliability alphas.

TABLE 5
Regression Results on Firm Strategy, Environment Factors, and Firm Performance in China

Variables	Patent Application	Domestic Market Share	External Orientation	Global New Product Sales	Domestic New Product Sales
Control Variables					
Firm Size	0.14*	−0.08	0.18**	−0.00	0.04
Total Assets	0.15*	−0.10	0.03	0.05	−0.01
Total Sales	−0.08	−0.07	0.03	0.02	0.04
Product Strategy					
Defender Strategy	−0.09*	0.06	−0.02	−0.05	0.08
Prospector Strategy	−0.02	0.12**	−0.01	0.02	−0.01
Environmental Factors					
Innovation Policy	0.03	−0.08	0.14**	0.20***	0.06
Professional Service	0.02	−0.02	−0.03	0.02	0.15**
Talent Market	0.11*	0.04	−0.10*	0.02	0.04
R&D Investment	0.01	−0.08	0.12**	0.22***	0.09
R^2	0.06	0.07	0.10	0.09	0.03
Adj. R^2	0.05	0.06	0.09	0.07	0.01
F-value	6.89***	10.10***	9.32***	5.02***	2.38*

Note: Total sample size $N = 725$; firm size: 1 = 300 employees or below, 2 = 300–2,000, 3 = 2,000 or above; total sales: 1 = RMB 30 million or below, 2 = RMB 30 million to 300 million, 3 = RMB 300 million or above; total assets: 1 = RMB 40 million or below, 2 = RMB 40 million to 400 million, 3 = RMB 400 million or above; corporate product strategies and environment factors are based on 5-point Likert scales; total R&D investments are standardized scores; domestic market share is based on a firm's market share ranking: 1 = No. 1 in market share, 2 = No. 2–5 in market share, 3 = No. 6–10 in market share, 4 = No. 11–50, and 5 = No. 50+.

Furthermore, Total R&D investment is found to be a significant predictor of firms' performance in their efforts to innovate products, in support of H2f. This study shows that R&D investment can improve a firm's global new product sales, the strongest effect among all examined relationships in this study. It also affects a firm's overseas market share as measured by external orientation.

DISCUSSION AND CONCLUSION

Product innovation is costly and risky for a firm, and successful launch of new products is, thus, crucially important to a firm's survival. While success factors studies have gained and retained great popularity in the past decades, most of prior academic work has been done within specific cultural contexts (Chua, Roth, and Lemoine 2015), focused on a particular product type, and usually provides only a short normative checklist of critical activities (Di Benedetto 1999; Dibrell, Craig, and Neubaum 2014; Ernst 2002). Recent research on success factors in product innovation has integrated prior research and called for a broader

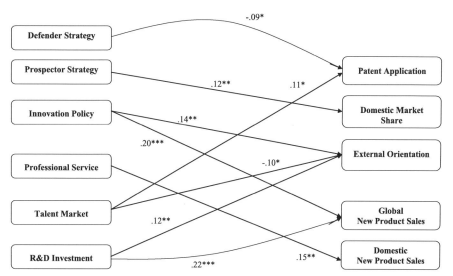

FIGURE 1. Firm Strategy, Environment Factors, and Firm Performance in China. The numbers along the lines are standardized betas; $*p < 0.05$, $**p < 0.01$, $***p$, 0.001 (two-tailed)

perspective to examine the relationship between product innovation strategy and firm performance (Dibrell et al. 2016; Fréchet and Goy 2017; Ma et al. 2015; Siguaw, Simpson, and Enz 2006; Sirén and Kohtamäki 2016).

By exploring what strategies and environment factors affect product innovation performance in the Chinese context, this study enriches the literature on success factors for product innovation across cultures, thereby building a more robust and integrated theory on product innovation and development applicable in a variety of contexts. With an indigenous perspective and using the developed measures for product innovation success factors and firm performance, this study provides empirical evidence for the critical roles of strategic choice, environment constraints, and R&D investment in improving overall firm performance in China's manufacturing sector.

In addition, instead of focusing on detailed technical contents of product innovation process, this study focuses on the broad picture of product strategy and its impact on overall firm performance, to echo the call for more integrated studies about success factors for new product development (Dahlander, O'Mahony, and Gann 2016; Ernst 2002; Ma et al. 2015; Song et al. 2011). As discussed in the introduction, while product innovation strategy was found the second most important success factor for new product development (Cooper and Kleinschmidt 1995b), product development and innovation strategy have rarely been examined in product innovation research in the past (Dibrell, Craig, and Neubaum 2014; Ernst 2002; Fréchet and Goy 2017; Song et al. 2011). This study specifically measures two types of product innovation strategy based on Chinese managers' own perceptions about their decision in initiating product innovation activities, and the results provide support for the important influence of product innovation strategy on firms' performance.

The study also considers the unique environmental context in China and its impact on product innovation and firm's performance. While environment factors have been widely studied (Cooper and Kleinschmidt 1995b, 1996; Song and Chen 2014), few of these factors are similar to the ones in China, as the Chinese economic and social system is so different from the ones in the West (Ma et al. 2015; Parry and Song 1994; Song and Parry 1994; Zhang, Hu, and Kotabe 2011). Based on Chinese managers' own definition of various environmental factors that are considered influential in the process of product innovation, a list of environment success factors for product innovation were compiled, which were, then, found in this study to be significantly related to overall firm performance, an important contribution to current literature on product innovation and new product development. It is surprising, though, that government regulations and infrastructure are not found to be related to any of the dependent variables, including patent application, domestic and global new product sales, market share, and external orientation.

The findings of this study also have important implications for managers. A good understanding of the relationship between product strategy, environmental constraints, and firm performance make it possible to help executives and policy makers create an environment conducive to facilitating product innovation in China. Based on the significant relationship between product innovation strategy, R&D investment, and firm performance, managers can create suitable strategies, or adjust R&D expenditure, in order to achieve their objectives, including patent application, global and domestic market share, or global new product sales.

Executives are also urged to go beyond single product development projects and look at the big picture in order to create effective product strategies and to improve overall firm's performance (Dibrell, Craig, and Neubaum 2014; Ernst 2002; Fréchet and Goy 2017). In the same vein, Chinese policy makers are encouraged to learn and adopt the findings of this study to make appropriate innovation policies, create supportive talent market, and establish reliable professional services in local environment, to help manufacturing firms innovate their products and increase their global and domestic sales. Managers in global multinationals can learn from the findings of this study how to better understand Chinese market and product innovation in China, so as to be better equipped with knowledge and practice when entering and competing in the Chinese market.

There are several limitations to the present study which should be taken into consideration in applying the results of this study to other contexts. Although we have a large sample of enterprises from various Chinese manufacturing firms, it is hard to argue that the selected sample is fully representative of the general population of Chinese manufacturing enterprises, a deficiency that limits the external validity of this study. Future research is encouraged to collect more data from other sectors in China to explore the generalizability of the findings of this study.

In addition, since this study is based on retrospective data, and managerial perceptions of key strategic choice and environment factors, more studies are needed to establish true cause-and-effect relationships between strategy and the environment and firms' performance. Future research is also called on to further explore the relationships between government regulations and infrastructure, and various firm performance variables, including patent application, domestic and global new product sales, market share, and external orientation, as government regulations and infrastructure are not found to be related to any of these perform-ance variables. Future research should explore the underlying cause of these findings.

This study uses a linear regression model to test the relationships. Future research may use experimental design or longitudinal methods to further investigate these relationships. Reliance on the respondents' feedback may also lead to the problem of common method bias. That being said, R&D investment, patent application, and various market shares and product sales are objective measures, and their significant interrelationships may implicitly support the validity of the methodology used in this study.

Another limitation of this study is that it explores a set of broad concepts and their interre-lationships at the organizational level. Executives might ask for more operational suggestions on how to generate product innovation, a question not answered in this study. Future research may try to integrate research both at the individual product level and at the organizational performance level, so that managers, by having sufficient technical details, can see the "product innovation tree," while not embroiled in too many details, so that they cannot see the "strategy and firm performance forest."

ORCID

Zhenzhong Ma (iD) http://orcid.org/0000-0003-3012-2810
Quan Jin (iD) http://orcid.org/0000-0001-8128-0048

REFERENCES

Beers, C., and F. Zand. 2014. "R&D Cooperation, Partner Diversity, and Innovation Performance: An Empirical Analysis." *Journal of Product Innovation Management* 31 (2):292–312. doi:10.1111/jpim.12096.

Brown, S. L., and K. M. Eisenhardt. 1995. "Product Development: Past Research, Present Findings, and Future Directions." *Academy of Management Review* 20 (2):343–78. doi:10.5465/amr.1995.9507312922.

Calantone, R. J., J. B. Schmidt, and M. Song. 1996. "Controllable Factors of New Product Success: A Cross-National Comparison." *Marketing Science* 15 (4):341–58. doi:10.1287/mksc.15.4.341.

Calantone, R. J., K. Chan, and A. S. Cui. 2006. "Decomposing Product Innovativeness and Its Effects on New Product Success." *Journal of Product Innovation Management* 23 (5):408–21. doi:10.1111/j.1540-5885.2006.00213.x.

Chua, R., Y. Roth, and J.-F. Lemoine. 2015. "The Impact of Culture on Creativity: How Cultural Tightness and Cultural Distance Affect Global Innovation Crowdsourcing Work." *Administrative Science Quarterly* 60 (2): 189–227. doi:10.1177/0001839214563595.

Cooper, R. G., and E. J. Kleinschmidt. 1995a. "Uncovering the Keys to New Product Success." *Engineering Management Review* 11 (4):315–37.

Cooper, R. G., and E. J. Kleinschmidt. 1995b. "Benchmarking the Firm's Critical Success Factors in New Product Development." *Journal of Product Innovation Management* 12 (5):374–91. doi:10.1016/0737-6782(95)00059-3.

Cooper, R. G., and E. J. Kleinschmidt. 1996. "Winning Businesses in Product Development: The Critical Success Factors." *Research Technology Management* 39 (4):18–29. doi:10.1080/08956308.1996.11671073.

Dahlander, Linus, Siobhan O'Mahony, and David M. Gann. 2016. "One Foot in, One Foot out: How Does Individuals' External Search Breadth Affect Innovation Outcomes?" *Strategic Management Journal* 37 (2): 280–302. doi:10.1002/smj.2342.

DeSarbo, W. S., A. Di Benedetto, M. Song, and I. Sinha. 2005. "Revisiting the Miles and Snow Strategic Framework: Uncovering Interrelationships between Strategic Types, Capabilities, Environmental Uncertainty, and Firm Performance." *Strategic Management Journal* 26 (1):47–74.

Di Benedetto, A. 1999. "Identifying the Key Success Factors in New Product Launch." *Journal of Product Innovation Management* 16 (6):530–44. doi:10.1016/S0737-6782(99)00014-4.

Dibrell, C., J. B. Craig, and D. O. Neubaum. 2014. "Linking the Formal Strategic Planning Process, Planning Flexibility, and Innovativeness to Firm Performance." *Journal of Business Research* 67 (9):2000–7. doi:10.1016/j.jbusres.2013.10.011.

DiMaggio, P. J., and W. W. Powell. 1983. "The Iron Cage Revisited: Institutional Isomorphism and Collective Rationality in Organizational Fields." *American Sociological Review* 48 (2):147–60. doi:10.2307/2095101.

Dyer, B., and M. Song. 1998. "Innovation Strategy and Sanctioned Conflict: A New Edge in Innovation?" *Journal of Product Innovation Management* 15 (6):505–19. doi:10.1016/S0737-6782(98)00032-0.

Ernst, H. 2002. "Success Factors of New Product Development: A Review of the Empirical Literature." *International Journal of Management Reviews* 4 (1):1–40. doi:10.1111/1468-2370.00075.

Ettlie, J. E., and M. Subramaniam. 2004. "Changing Strategies and Tactics for New Product Development." *Journal of Product Innovation Management* 21 (2):95–109. doi:10.1111/j.0737-6782.2004.00060.x.

Fréchet, M., and H. Goy. 2017. "Does Strategy Formalization Foster Innovation? Evidence from a French Sample of Small to Medium-Sized Enterprises." *Management* 20 (3):266–86. doi:10.3917/mana.203.0266.

Gatignon, H., and J.-M. Xuereb. 1997. "Strategic Orientation of the Firm and New Product Performance." *Journal of Marketing* 34 (1):77–90. doi:10.1177/002224379703400107.

Grewal, R., and R. Dharwadkar. 2002. "The Role of the Institutional Environment in Marketing Channels." *Journal of Marketing* 66 (3):82–97. doi:10.1509/jmkg.66.3.82.18504.

Griffin, A. 1997. "PDMA Research on New Product Development Practices: Updating Trends and Benchmarking Best Practices." *Journal of Product Innovation Management* 14 (6):429–58. doi:10.1016/S0737-6782(97)00061-1.

Guan, J., R. Yam, E. Tang, and A. Lau. 2009. "Innovation Strategy and Performance during Economic Transition: Evidences in Beijing, China." *Research Policy* 38 (5):802–12. doi:10.1016/j.respol.2008.12.009.

Kamasak, R. 2015. "Determinants of Innovation Performance: A Resource-Based Study." *Procedia - Social and Behavioral Sciences* 195:1330–7. doi:10.1016/j.sbspro.2015.06.311.

Lichtenthaler, U., and H. Ernst. 2007. "Opening up the Innovation Process: The Role of Technology Aggressiveness." *R&D Management* 39 (1):38–54. doi:10.1111/j.1467-9310.2008.00522.x.

Ma, Z., and Y. Lee. 2008. "Patent Application and Technological Collaboration in Inventive Activities: 1980-2005." *Technovation* 28 (6):379–90. doi:10.1016/j.technovation.2007.07.011.

Ma, Z., M. Yu, C. Gao, J. Zhou, and Z. Yang. 2015. "Institutional Constraints of Product Innovation in China: Evidence from International Joint Ventures." *Journal of Business Research* 68 (5):949–56. doi:10.1016/j.jbusres.2014.09.022.

Ma, Z., Y. Lee, and C. Chen. 2009. "Booming or Emerging? China's Technological Capability and International Collaboration in Patent Activities." *Technological Forecasting & Social Change* 76 (6):787–96. doi:10.1016/j.techfore.2008.11.003.

Miles, R. E., and C. C. Snow. 1978. *Organizational Strategy, Structure, and Process.* New York: McGraw-Hill.

Parry, M. E., and M. Song. 1994. "Identifying New Product Successes in China." *Journal of Product Innovation Management* 11 (1):15–30. doi:10.1016/0737-6782(94)90116-3.

Prescott, J. E. 1986. "Environments as Moderators of the Relationship between Strategy and Performance." *Academy of Management Journal* 29 (2):329–46. doi:10.5465/256191.

Pullen, A., P. De Weerd-Nederhof, A. Groen, M. Song, and O. Fisscher. 2009. "Successful Patterns of Internal SME Characteristics Leading to High Overall Innovation Performance." *Creativity and Innovation Management* 18 (3):209–23. doi:10.1111/j.1467-8691.2009.00530.x.

Scott, W. R. 2008. *Institutions and Organizations: Ideas and Interests.* Los Angeles, CA: Sage Publications.

Siguaw, J. A., P. M. Simpson, and C. A. Enz. 2006. "Conceptualizing Innovation Orientation: A Framework for Study and Integration of Innovation Research." *Journal of Product Innovation Management* 23 (6):556–74. doi:10.1111/j.1540-5885.2006.00224.x.

Sirén, C., and M. Kohtamäki. 2016. "Stretching Strategic Learning to the Limit: The Interaction between Strategic Planning and Learning." *Journal of Business Research* 69 (2):653–63. doi:10.1016/j.jbusres.2015.08.035.

Song, L. Z., M. Song, and A. Di Benedetto. 2009. "A Staged Service Innovation Model." *Decision Sciences* 40 (3):571–99. doi:10.1111/j.1540-5915.2009.00240.x.

Song, M., and J. Noh. 2006. "Best New Product Development and Management Practices in the Korean High-Tech Industry." *Industrial Marketing Management* 35 (3):262–78. doi:10.1016/j.indmarman.2005.04.007.

Song, M., and M. E. Parry. 1994. "The Dimensions of Industrial New Product Success and Failure in State Enterprises in the People's Public of China." *Journal of Product Innovation Management* 11 (2):105–18. doi: 10.1111/1540-5885.1120105.

Song, M., and M. E. Parry. 1996. "What Separates Japanese New Product Winners from Losers?" *Journal of Product Innovation Management* 13 (5):422–39. doi:10.1016/0737-6782(96)00055-0.

Song, M., and M. E. Parry. 1997a. "A Cross-National Comparative Study of New Product Development Processes: Japan and the United States." *Journal of Marketing* 61 (2):1–18. doi:10.2307/1251827.

Song, M., and M. E. Parry. 1997b. "The Determinants of Japanese New Product Successes." *Journal of Marketing Research* 34 (1):64–76.

Song, M., and M. M. Montoya-Weiss. 2001. "The Effect of Perceived Technological Uncertainty on Japanese New Product Development." *Academy of Management Journal* 44 (1):61–80. doi:10.2307/3069337.

Song, M., and Y. Chen. 2014. "Organizational Attributes, Market Growth, and Product Innovation." *Journal of Product Innovation Management* 31 (6):1312–29. doi:10.1111/jpim.12185.

Song, M., A. Di Benedetto, and Y. L. Zhao. 1999. "Pioneering Advantages in Manufacturing and Service Industries: Empirical Evidence from Nine Countries." *Strategic Management Journal* 20 (9):811–36. doi:10.1002/(SICI)1097-0266(199909)20:9<811::AID-SMJ52>3.0.CO;2-#.

Song, M., S. Im, H. van der Bij, and L. Z. Song. 2011. "Does Strategic Planning Enhance or Impede Innovation and Firm Performance?" *Journal of Product Innovation Management* 28 (4):503–20. doi:10.1111/j.1540-5885.2011.00822.x.

Song, M., T. Kawakami, and A. Stringfellow. 2010. "A Cross-National Comparative Study of Senior Management Policy, Marketing-Manufacturing Involvement, and Innovation Performance." *Journal of Product Innovation Management* 27 (2):179–200. doi:10.1111/j.1540-5885.2010.00709.x.

Souder, W. E., and M. Song. 1997. "Contingent Product Design and Marketing Strategies Influencing New Product Success and Failure in U.S. and Japanese Electronics Firms." *Journal of Product Innovation Management* 14 (1): 21–34. doi:10.1016/S0737-6782(96)00079-3.

Souder, W. E., and M. Song. 1998. "Analyses of U.S. and Japanese Management Processes Associated with New Product Success and Failure in High and Low Familiarity Markets." *Journal of Product Innovation Management* 15 (3):208–23. doi:10.1016/S0737-6782(97)00079-9.

Subramaniam, M. 2006. "Integrating Cross-Border Knowledge for Transnational New Product Development." *Journal of Product Innovation Management* 23 (6):541–55. doi:10.1111/j.1540-5885.2006.00223.x.

Subramaniam, M., and N. Venkatraman. 2001. "Determinants of Transnational New Product Development Capability: Testing the Influence of Transferring and Deploying Tacit Overseas Knowledge." *Strategic Management Journal* 22 (4):359–78. doi:10.1002/smj.163.

Subramaniam, M., S. R. Rosenthal, and K. J. Hatten. 1998. "Global New Product Development Process: Preliminary Findings and Research Propositions." *Journal of Management Studies* 35 (6):773–96. doi:10.1111/1467-6486.00119.

Xie, J., M. Song, and A. Stringfellow. 2003. "Antecedents and Consequences of Goal Incongruity on New Product Development in Five Countries: A Marketing View." *Journal of Product Innovation Management* 20 (3):233–50. doi:10.1111/1540-5885.2003005.

Zhang, D., P. Hu, and M. Kotabe. 2011. "Marketing-Industrial Design Integration in New Product Development: The Case of China." *Journal of Product Innovation Management* 28 (3):360–73. doi:10.1111/j.1540-5885.2011.00803.x.

Index

Note: Figures are indicated by *italics* and tables by **bold** type.

innovation 37; local firms 32, 33, 35, 36, 39–41; local governments interfere and intervene 38; MNCs 36, 37; types of 41
International Subsidiary 40
iPad® 81
Irico Group 99

Jacoby, Jacob 74
Jin, Quan 4
Jorge A. 3
Joshi, A. 87, 88

Kaplan, Leon B. 74
Kellermans, F. 8
Kirton, M. 78
knowledge intensive industry 44, **44**
Konka Group 99

labor-intensive industry 44, **44**
Lance, C. E. 44
Lan, Fusheng 12–14, 18, 19
latecomer firms 8–11
"leapfrogging" 20
LeFebvre, Stephen 14
Lenovo 99
leverage: of industry linkages 15–17; of international linkages 17–18
liability of localness 36
Li, H. 44
linear regression model 109
linkage-leverage-learning (LLL) framework: archival material 12; BioVittoria 12–13, 23, 24; dragon multinationals 7, 9, 24; emerging economies 6; Gioia, Corley and Hamilton 12; Guilin GFS Bio-Tech 12–13, 23; Guilin GFS Monk Fruit Corporation 7, 12–13, 29–30 (*see also* Monk Fruit Corporation); individual and organizational resources 21; innovation, international markets 20; internationalization 8; latecomer firms 8–11; "leapfrogging" 20; local and foreign 21; MNE 7; model of institutions and innovation *25*; Mr. Fusheng Lan 12; organizational innovation 22; politico-economic policy 21; pre-conceptualization of issues 11; RBV 8; resources 8; single in-depth case study 11; Sino-foreign collaboration 24; strategic and organizational innovation 22; strategic and structural innovations 22–3; strategic networks 24–5; strategy of bricolage 11
local firms 32, 33, 35, 36, 39–41
logistic regression analyses **64**; robustness test **65**
Lu, J. 24
Luo Han Guo (monk fruit) 13, 15

marketing strategy 72
"Mass Entrepreneurship and Innovation by All" 53, 94
Mathews, J. A. 7, 9, 12, 21, 23
Ma, Zhenzhong 4
Mccann, B. 57, 62

Mendi, P. 57
mergers and acquisitions (M&As) linkages 11
Meyer, K. 9
Microsoft® 79
Miles, R. E. 97, 102
Misangyi, V. F. 87, 88
Mitchell, V. M. 78
Mitchell, V. W. 77
Mobile World Congress 72
Monk Fruit Corporation 13–15, 19, 21, 22; BioVittoria 13, 14–15; Chinese agro-business 13–14; GRAS notification program 13; Guangxi Province, China 13; Guilin Bio-DaDi 13; Guilin GFS Bio-Tech Joint Venture 14–15; high intensive sweeteners 13; Innovation and Intellectual Property **16**; leverage of industry linkages 15–17; leverage of international linkages 17–18; linkage, leverage and learning **29–30**; linkages, leverage and learning 14; organizational innovation 19–20; organizational learning through linkages 18–19; South America 13
Morris, David Z. 31
multinational corporations (MNCs) 1, 4, 36–8, 48, 97
multinational enterprise (MNE) 6–11, 20–3, **30**, 65
multiple imputation (MI) 61
Murray, K. B. 74

National Bureau of Statistics of China (NBSC) 101
"natural sweetener" 12
Nearest Neighbor (NN) matching algorithm 40
NECTRESSE™ 18
new product development (NPD) 59, 62
New Zealand 11, 13–15, 17, 19

ongoing information: search behavior 81
ownership advantage theory 2
Ownership-Location-Internationalization (OLI) paradigm 8, 9, 33, 46

Parnell, J. 57
perceived risk 3–4, 72, 73; configurations of 76; consumers' purchase decisions 72; factor analysis **82**; impact of 87; independent measurement 82–3; and information search 73–4, 89; ongoing search 77–9; pre-purchase search 79–80; relevancy of demographics 77
Peréz, Jorge Heredia 3
Phillips, L. W. 77
politico-economic policy, Chinese government 21
Portis, B. 81
pre-purchase information 79, 87, 88; configurations 85–6; search behavior 81–2
Product Development and Management Association (PDMA) 75
product innovation: Chinese manufacturing firms **100**, 108; conceptual framework 95–8; data collection 99–101; direct relevance and inherent appeal 94; environmental constraints, China